W9-AAP-697

Y. OVSYANNIKOV

RUSSIAN FOLK ARTS AND CRAFTS

PROGRESS PUBLISHERS • MOSCOW •

Translated from the Russian by
A. Shkarovsky

Designed by
S. Pozharsky and N. Glazunova

The photographs by D. Smirnov,
M. Uspensky and others reproduce
exhibits on display at the Moscow Museum
of Art and the Historical Museum.

Юрий Овсянников

РУССКОЕ НАРОДНОЕ ДЕКОРАТИВНОЕ
ИСКУССТВО

На английском языке

CONTENTS

IN LIEU OF A PREFACE

happened to be spending the night in a small village on the eastern bank of the Volga many miles from the nearest railway station. It was autumn and dusk had already fallen. The wind whined and howled and rain lashed the roof.

My kind host urged me to draw more tea, piping hot, from the samovar, as we talked of practically everything under the sun. However, I broke off almost in the middle of a word, when I heard his wife, Agrafena, seemingly totally oblivious of her husband, myself and the boiling samovar, leisurely recount the following captivating fairy-tale, as she put her granddaughter Nastya to sleep.

*

Once upon a time there was an orphan girl, called Maryushka. She was a very nice girl, quiet, modest, and well-behaved. No one in those parts could do embroidery as well as she. She worked with coloured silks and glass beads, making a shirt for one, a towel for another, and a pretty sash for someone else. She was always well content with what money she got which was her only means.

Her fame as a skilled embroideress reached the ears of merchants living beyond the seas. They came from afar to see her handiwork. They gazed, wonder-struck, never having expected to find anything so beautiful.

One after another, they tried to persuade Maryushka to come with them, promising her riches galore, but the girl would reply:

"I do not need riches and I shall never leave the village where I was born. However, I am willing to sell my handiwork to all who find it to their taste."

*With that the merchants had to be content.
They left, spreading the story of her skill to all
the ends of the earth, until one day it
reached the ear of the ogre Kashchey the Immortal,
who waxed wroth on learning there was such a
beauty in the world that he had never
seen.
He at once assumed the form of a handsome youth
and winged his way over deep oceans and tall
mountains till he came to Maryushka's
cottage.
He knocked at the door and bowed to her
as was the custom. Then he asked to see the
needlework she had completed. Maryushka set out
shirts and towels, each more beautiful
than the other.
"Kind sir," said she, "may it please you to
take anything you wish. If you have not the money
now, you may pay me later, when you have money
to spare. But should my work not find
favour in your eyes, please tell me why and
also what to do. Be assured that I shall
do my best."
Her kind words and the sight of all that beauty
made Kashchey angrier still. How was it
possible for a plain country girl to make things
finer than he, the great Kashchey the Immortal,
himself possessed. In wheedling tones
he said:
"Come with me, Maryushka. I will make you
queen. You will live in a palace built of precious
gems. You will eat off gold, and sleep on eider
down. You will walk in an orchard
where birds of paradise sing sweetly and golden apples
grow."
"Do not speak so, kind sir," Maryushka replied.*

"I need neither your riches, nor your strange marvels. There is no sweeter place than the fields and woods where one was born. I shall never leave this village, where my parents lie buried, and where live the folk to whom my needlework brings joy. I shall never embroider for you alone."

The ogre was furious at this answer. "Because you are so loth to take leave of your kindred, a bird you shall be, and no more a maiden fair," he cried.

And in an instant, a Fire-Bird flapped its wings where Maryushka had stood. Kashchey became a black eagle, and soared into the skies, to swoop down on the Fire-Bird. Grasping her tight in his cruel talons, he carried her above the clouds.

As soon as Maryushka felt the power in those steel claws and realised she was being taken away, she resolved to leave a last memory of herself.

She shed her brilliant plumage and feather after feather floated down to fall on meadow and forest. And though the mischievous wind covered the feathers with grass and leaves, nothing could rob them of their glowing, rainbow colours.

As the feathers fell, Maryushka's strength ebbed. Though the Fire-Bird died in the black eagle's talons, her feathers continued to live, down on the ground. They were not ordinary feathers but magic ones which only those who loved beauty, and whose hands sought to make beautiful things for others, could see and admire.

"Grannie," Nastya interjected. "Because
Grandpa painted those bright wooden platters,
does that mean he has seen Maryushka's
feathers?"
"Yes, love. That is why he has the gift for painting.
However, it's high time you closed your eyes
and fell asleep."
... Nastya had fallen asleep long ago. My hosts
were snoring gently on the bedding above their big
tiled stove. But I couldn't close my eyes.
The fairy-tale I had overheard kept running through
my head. I recollected something said by that
great Russian writer Maxim Gorky. "Man is
an artist by nature," he had observed. "In
everything he does he tries in one way or another
to make life beautiful."
Russian handiwork has always served both
utilitarian and aesthetic purposes. Every
peasant cottage had its delicate tracery
of ornament. The back of every sleigh and the wheels
of every cart were gaily painted. Various
household utensils and the craftsman's tools,
such as jack-planes, laundry beetles,
flails and distaffs, were beautifully carved.
However, it was in holiday attire that a particular
effort was made to achieve perfection. Such
was the wish of Maryushka and the hundreds
of her anonymous sisters and brothers who had seen
the feathers of the fabulous
Fire-Bird.
"Art was fathered," Maxim Gorky wrote,
"by the potters, the blacksmiths and goldsmiths,
the weavers, masons, and carpenters,
the carvers in wood and ivory, the armourers,
the house painters, and the
dressmakers."

While striving for decorative excellence, the craftsman never foreswore the utilitarian purpose of the article he made. Over the centuries he evolved the best and handiest form of household article. In turn, the form prompted the ornamentation.

Examine closely the wooden vases with their intricate floral patterns fashioned by the craftsmen of Khokhloma. Notice that the flowers are smaller at the tapering foot, and bigger and brighter on the swollen middle section of the vases. This is not fortuitous; the wider part attracts the eye before the stem and foot.

Or observe the carved pattern on a Kholmogory ivory dressing-table casket. The lid, as the element chiefly visible, bears the openwork picture of gambolling reindeer, while the walls, seen only when one picks up the box, have but a simple pattern.

Very often it is the medium that suggests the form. Thus, the carved, white, unpainted wooden toy must have a clear-cut silhouette, so that the animal or human character depicted be readily recognisable. When working in clay, the peasant artist produced a stylised form, as this fragile material ruled out intricate detail. The conventionalised form naturally demanded a conventionalised colouring.

The village craftsman borrowed themes and decorative motifs from the natural environment, and from folk tales and beliefs.

The centuries-old experience amassed by the folk craftsmen tremendously influenced the development of professional art. A legion of illustrious architects, sculptors, painters and composers have viewed popular art as a treasure chamber providing an inexhaustible store of imagery and themes for their own work. Suffice it to mention the paintings of Surikov and Vasnetsov, the architecture of Bazhenov and Shchusev, and the music of Chaikovsky, Mussorgsky and Rimsky-Korsakov—to mention but a few.

Today we are witnessing the natural fusion of folk and professional art. Folk craftsmen turn professional, while college-trained sculptors and painters devote themselves to the folk arts and handicrafts—an interplay that serves the decorative arts handsomely.

The following chapters will tell something of the glorious history of the Russian folk arts, of true craftsmen and their masterpieces.

WOOD CARVING

A MIRACLE OF TRANSFORMATION

The Story Historians Tell

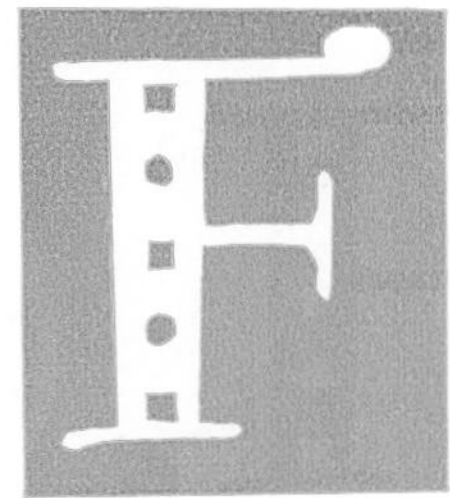or eight centuries this wooden head, the size of a small fist, lay buried in the earth. Though time has robbed it of its colouring, the narrowed eyes and the sardonic grin that still hovers about the slit of a mouth, as if mocking the archaeologists, seem to say: "Well, you've discovered me, all right, but just try to find out who made me!"

Indeed, though the head was found many years ago, we still don't know who made it. However, scholars have not lost hope. Perhaps in a year or two, they will unearth a twin to this carved head, with the name of its maker just discernible in a cobweb of minute cracks. After all some objects have borne the inscription "Made by Buris". In another case, "This is Semyon's hone" was written on its antique wooden handle. A letter on birch bark was discovered almost at the same time as the wooden head. How many more mysteries the ancient Russian town of Novgorod still conceals, is a question nobody can answer.

Novgoroders have grown accustomed to the hum and clamour coming from beyond the tall wooden fence that has been put up in the heart of their town. At the bottom of the huge excavation pit dozens of people closely scrutinise every handful of clay and sand. These are archaeologists seeking to solve the riddles history propounds, and hunting for finds that would tell of the past. Because though much is already known, still more remains to be unravelled.

Paradoxically enough, the earth of Novgorod itself lends a helping hand. Its moistness prevents wooden articles from rotting and preserves them intact in both their original form and size. Some of these wooden objects have enabled scholars to clarify a few vague points germane to the history of one of Russia's oldest towns.

In the summer of 1951 Professor Artemi Artsykhovsky's team of archaeologists discovered a wooden chalice with a lovely pattern of two

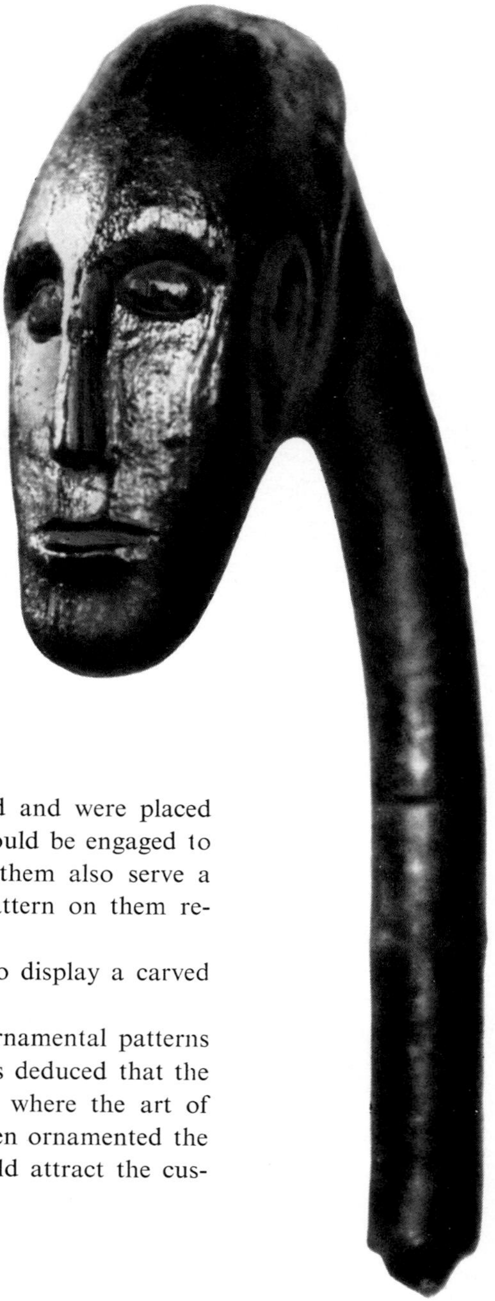

16 *Man's head, 12th century, Novgorod. One of the oldest existing specimens of ancient Russian wooden sculpture*

fancifully interlacing tendrils carved in relief. The questions it posed were: When was it made? Where? And how typical was the ornamental pattern?

The first question was soon answered. The depth at which the chalice was found, other objects discovered at this spot, and the style of carving suggested that the find was some 900 years old. As for the second question, a comparison of the pattern with church adornments and illuminated manuscripts warranted the conclusion that its author had been a wood carver of Novgorod.

The third question was answered only several years later when huge wooden pillars and the remains of carved furniture were found. Pillars like these supported the central beam in the bigger houses of Novgorod and were placed right in the middle of the room. A master carver would be engaged to ornament them from top to bottom, thus making them also serve a second purpose, that of interior decoration. The pattern on them resembled that on the chalice.

The remains of chairs and benches discovered also display a carved interlace.

By carefully comparing the style of carving and ornamental patterns used on all the wooden objects found, archaeologists deduced that the chalice pattern was quite typical of old Novgorod, where the art of wood carving had attained great perfection. Craftsmen ornamented the most ordinary utilitarian objects in a way that would attract the customer's fancy.

In that case the question arises: If the carvers were so skilful, why has only one wooden sculpture been found so far?

The celebrated 10th-century Arab traveller Ibn Fadlan has handed down a description of the Slavonic idols that used to be carved from tree trunks. There is mention of wooden images of pagan deities also in that ancient Russian chronicle *Povesti Vremennykh Let* (The Chronicles of Contemporary Years). "And when Prince Vladimir was enthroned in Kiev, he placed on the hilltop a wooden Perun and idols of Dazhbog and Stribog," the scribe wrote. Excavation of ancient Slavonic shrines has brought to light remains of idols dating back to the 9th-10th centuries.

Consequently, wooden figures of human beings had been carved extensively in old Russia before the 10th century. Why then, in spite of every effort, have archaeologists so far found only one wooden head?

Christianity was adopted in pagan Russia in 989. This was an important step forward both in the consolidation of the country's statehood and its

"Interlace." Traditional Russian ornamental motif on 11th-century Novgorod wooden chalice

St. Paraskeva. Of anonymous workmanship. Mid-16th century

Right: detail

St. Nicholas of Mozhaisk, 16th century. This flat effigy demonstrates an ignorance in dimensional carving

Painted folding altar with St. Nicholas of Mozhaisk.
Flap depict St. Boris and St. Gleb

cultural advancement. However, the church demanded that all pagan idols be destroyed. Any attempt to carve a wooden or stone statue was harshly persecuted as heresy. True, a few score years later, the church was obliged to employ sculptors and thereby hangs a tale.

St. Eupraxia of Good Friday was honoured as the patroness of all wells and springs. Her icons were nailed up at every well and spring to serve as a constant reminder of the "saint" who had so graciously condescended to bestow the blessing of water on the human race. However, in the rain, snow and heat, the paint flaked off and the icons had to be renewed frequently. To remedy the situation, the church commanded sculptors to carve statues that would stand up to the elements, to take the place of the icons. Exhibited in many museums today are rudely hewn wooden images of the saint.

Growing aware of the axiomatic truth that the people's creative genius cannot be kept forever in duress, the church, whose rule by now was firmly established, allowed craftsmen to carve icons in relief and statues of the "saints".

A wooden sculpture of the late 14th century is now displayed at the Tretyakov Art Gallery in Moscow—a statue of St. Nicholas holding a sword in one hand and a small fortress in the other.

Hundreds of years later, Russian craftsmen again tried carving human figures from wood. An anonymous attempt to reproduce one of the many icon portraits of St. Nicholas in wood resulted in an image practically devoid of the third dimension, even though it was carved out of the trunk of an oak. However with every decade the folk carvers were slowly amassing experience and regaining their lost skills.

However, as soon as a master craftsman treated of mundane themes, he was persecuted and his work disfigured. When the Englishman Christopher Galloway embellished the extra tier added to the Kremlin's Spasskaya Tower with four nudes of mythological personages, the figures were clothed in kaftans to save the devout embarrassment. "There were made cloth cassocks for four statues," the chronicler tells us, "for which twelve arshins (one arshin= 28 inches) of English cloth of diverse colours were used." Since this was not the only case in the mid-17th century of mundane statuary, the Church appealed to believers to refrain from adorning roofs and gates with carved images of people, animals, and centaurs.

St. George, 17th century. Northern Russia.
A fine blend of ornate carving and painting ▶

Evangelists, mid-18th century. From a village church in Tambov Region in Central Russia

King David plucking a dulcimer. Early 18th century. Painted wood. Smolensk

Right: detail

Bird-shaped handsaw handle, 1836

Jack-plane with carved crouching lion. Of anonymous workmanship. About 150 years old

Distaffs from Archangel and Kostroma regions. Colour schemes and patterns show a pronounced regionality

 Only at the tail end of the 17th century did Peter the Great officially sanction the erection of monuments and decorative statuary in gardens and parks.

Despite the Russian Orthodox Church's bitter campaign over the ages against heresy and pagan beliefs, the echoes of remote, almost forgotten worship continued to live on in folk rites and customs, and in the folk arts and handicrafts, including woodwork.

In parts of Gorky region, on the Volga's wooded left bank, one may still find cottages ornamented with woodwork done in relief. Inset in the intricate, lush floral pattern on the eaves, is the figure of a mermaid or shore-woman—centuries ago, in the now-forgotten beliefs of the ancient Slavs, protectress of meadows, ploughlands and hearths. Another of the principal deities was the Sun-God, who was depicted usually as a circle or as a symbolic flaming-red horse sometimes possessing three heads. With the advent of Christianity the sun symbol fused with the image of the biblical prophet of Elijah being borne aloft in his chariot by three horses. Carved images of horse heads—supposedly able to ward off trouble and the evil eye—still continue to decorate many a rooftree.

The horse, or rather its head, was also depicted in carved wooden ware. Even today in a village in Vologda or Archangel regions, the kind housewife will serve the thirsty traveller a drink of refreshing spring water in a carved dipper bearing a resemblance to a floating duck and having a horse head for its handle.

Still more popular was the circle, the other symbol of the Sun-God. Having been transformed with time into a fanciful rosette, it came to adorn the back of a bench, the frame of a mirror, the laundry beetle, and the distaff. The distaff, incidentally, was held in particular esteem by the peasant. Vologda village ancients have told me that flax represents sunbeams, while its flowers are blue because they have ingested the azure of summer skies. The distaff used for the spinning of flax is no common object. Its beauty was an indication of the material standards of its owners. Held in great repute were the distaffs of Kostroma and Yaroslavl, whose delicate pierced tracery reminds one of lace.

The wealth of fantasy displayed by folk carvers in their undeviating subliminal adherence to ancient tradition leaves one amazed. Thus, Russian folk craftsmen have traditionally handed down through the ages, from generation to generation, the image of the lion, whose antecedents no one really knows. The noble beast is found on 12th-century copper buckles from Novgorod, on

the cathedral of St. Demetrius in Vladimir, on carved 15th-century wooden icons, on 18th-century peasant cottages, and even on the handle of a jack-plane that is a mere 100 years old.

It is to be regretted that most folk craftsmen remain anonymous. Seldom will one find in time-yellowed archives even a cursory mention of a carver who had been commanded to work under contract. It was still rarer for the carver to initial his creations. Only a very talented craftsman would do that in the realisation that he stood head and shoulders above his brother carvers.

Early 20th-century historians were able to establish the name of only one of the most gifted master carvers of the past. They discovered on a small, superbly executed wooden icon the inscription "Made in the summer of 6964 (that is 1450), in the reign of Grand Prince Vasily Vasilyevich at Troitse-Sergievsky Monastery at the bidding of Superior Vasian by the hand of the lay monk Ambrosius."

Founded in 1337, Troitse-Sergievsky Monastery, one of the biggest and richest in Muscovy (now the Troitse-Sergievsky Monastery in the town of Zagorsk, Moscow Region), soon developed into a centre of folk arts and handicrafts.

Vodka flask, 1818. Such articles were carved in wood too

The name of the monk Ambrosius is mentioned in the monastery's chronicles again in 1491, by which time he had risen to the position of its treasurer.

"Impious Doll"

THIS talented craftsman can most likely be considered the founder of a whole school of monastery carvers, who were celebrated right up to 1917 for their boxwood icons. Gradually, as the years rolled by, a wood-carving industry developed in the surrounding villages on the monasterial estates, with whole hamlets—Bogorodskoye for example—devoting themselves to the craft. Since the peasant could not make his small plot feed himself and his family, he was obliged to look for an additional source of income. He naturally turned to carving, as the numerous pilgrims flocking to the neighbouring monastery sought to take away with them some souvenir of their visit—a spoon, box, cross, or religious miniature.

The money accruing from the sale of these peasant souvenirs swelled the coffers of the monastery. At first the holy fathers praised Ambrosius to the high heavens, until one day they received a nasty shock. It was clay that was to blame.

In the early 19th century a deposit of clay suitable for the making of chinaware was discovered some one hundred versts outside Zagorsk. Soon dozens of smaller and bigger manufactories mushroomed in the local villages, some, subsequently, to gain world repute.

In addition to tableware, practically all the potteries produced diverse figurines. These objects attracted the peasant craftsmen, who attempted to imitate the more interesting of them. In turn, the potters

"Autocracy." Wooden toy carved during the First Russian Revolution of 1905

"Family of Bogorodskoye Master-carvers at Work", early 20th century. By A. Chushkin

asked the wood carvers to model hard wood prototypes for their china miniatures. Thus a statuette originally done in porcelain, would be followed by its sister in wood, or vice versa. An interesting story is told of the time.

On June 18, 1822, the Russian tsar's cabinet of ministers met to discuss a question of state importance, that of the "impious doll". Archimandrite Savva of Saratov Monastery had reported that in November 1821 he had seen at a town fair the china statuette of a monk carrying on his back a young girl concealed in a sheaf of straw. This, he maintained, was "defamation of the clergy". The cabinet referred the matter to tsar Alexander I. An imperial edict was issued confiscating and forbidding possession of the statuette, and tendering thanks to the archimandrite.

34 This figurine was made at merchant Khrapunov's potteries in the village of Kuzayevo of Moscow Province. Its wooden sister depicted the same lascivious monk with the girl in the sheaf.

It is hard to say which of the two appeared first. However, other satirical pieces in wood, that are to be seen at the museum in Zagorsk, show that the peasant craftsmen were fond of having a good laugh at the expense of their spiritual fathers.

Painted wooden figures, dating back to the middle 19th century, of concertina playing corpulent monks, their faces crimson from strong drink, and of obviously pregnant nuns are on display.

However, not only the clergy were satirised by the craftsmen of Bogorodskoye but feather-brained, vain barinyas (gentlewomen), snobbish officers, and greedy merchants also received their share of ridicule. No wonder the barinya series were known in the trade as the "Dury", the "sillies". The 15-inch figure was usually carved from a prism-shaped block of wood, the widest side serving

Cooper, late 19th century. By A. Chushkin

as the back. The other two sides were modelled into the round, button-nosed face of a fat, complacent gentlewoman. Though the arms, shoulders, waist and breast were conventionalised to the extreme, the dress was a faithful copy of the fashions in vogue in the first half of the past century.

Stylised to the same degree, was the philandering coxcomb of a hussar, who was often depicted reclining, arms akimbo, against a pillar, with a spy-glass held in his right hand.

The vagaries of fashion among the titled rich were often caricatured by peasant craftsmen. When horse-riding became the craze with provincial belles, they were at once depicted in riding habits astride a . . . rooster.

Now and then, the good-humoured grin yielded to outright satire. At the time of the 1905 revolution, a daring caricature was fashioned, depicting a

Urban scene, late 19th century. By A. Chushkin

*"Dinner in the Field"
Menage by D. Baras-
kov. Second half
19th century*

"Old Woman with Distaff and Old Man Plaiting Bast Shoes." Bogorodskoye. About 200 years old

trio of squat, obese gendarmes supporting on their heads a throne of evil-snarling monsters on top of which sat a pot-bellied tsar holding a bottle of vodka in one hand and a huge church candle in the other.

Naturally, the authorities at once banned the hawking of this toy. However, the clever craftsmen found a way out. They sold each figure separately, affording

"Blacksmiths." Old animated toy

their customer the amusing opportunity of gluing together the whole group himself.

The technique used to manufacture these sculptural miniatures is reflected in woodwork itself. In the early 1900s, A. Chushkin, a craftsman of Bogorodskoye, modelled in limewood a group showing master carvers at work.

It is a winter evening. The smoky wick sheds a faint glow. The housewife hums a sad tune as she spins. The head of the family and his elder son lean over the low joiner's bench, busily carving. Behind them kneels the younger son, chopping a store of blocks. Though the tired boy can hardly keep his eyes open, he knows he must not fall asleep, but help the family to earn money.

Objects relating to life in Bogorodskoye were made by other craftsmen too. As a matter of fact, every occasion was depicted. Captured forever in wood are such scenes as the flogging of a peasant, the chopping of wood, a carpenter at work, lunching in the field, threshing, and returning from mowing—to mention a few. Of particular interest is the "Village Assembly" group, which most faithfully conveys the atmosphere in the Russian village towards the close of the past century. In the centre stands the village elder in town clothes. Close to him are square-bearded rich farmers in highboots and peaked caps. On the fringes are the village poor in bast sandals and ragged smocks.

Though harassed and hampered, the village carvers elevated the once forbidden mundane folk sculpture to the heights of a genuine fine art. In this painstaking, yet worthwhile, effort, a great role was played by the ordinary children's toy.

Whether of royal lineage or humble peasant stock, boys and girls of every nation and epoch have always loved toys, and no parent would ever deny them to his child.

The carved wooden toy of Russia first received written mention in 1636, when palace records noted that "a toy cart with wooden horses" had been purchased from the Trinity Sergius Monastery for the royal children.

The next mention is found 85 years later, when in 1721, Catherine, Empress of Peter the Great, acquired from the monastery a whole set including "three cows, two horses, two deer, two rams, two pairs of swans, two roosters, one duck with three ducklings, and a town with soldiers."

From the meagre scraps of information contained in the Empress's expense accounts scholars have been able to trace the ancestry of the wooden toy, so great a favourite with children today.

These figures were made with the aid of such simple peasant tools as the axe, knife, and sundry chisels. Doing no preliminary moulding or sketching, the craftsman lopped off a block of wood, determining the size and shape by rule of thumb. Then with the chisel he shaved off superfluous wood, completing the toy with a knife as sharp as a razor blade.

Though his tools were crude, the craftsman demonstrated a surprising faculty for conveying the salient characteristic of the beast or bird chosen.

A child tires quickly of even the loveliest of dolls, when it is static, immobile. The craftsman, who had children of his own, realised this, and thus there appeared the animated toy. Affixed separately to two small joined pieces are a peasant and a bear. But alternately pushing and pulling the pieces, the man and animal are made to strike alternately at the anvil with their heavy mallets, and thus work in rhythm like real blacksmiths.

Another kind of animated toy is one of a whole group of animals or people mounted on a jointed "trellis", with a scissor or concertina-like movement. In Russian this toy is known as the "razvod", which means literally "moving apart". Indeed, again by pushing and pulling, a herd of cattle can be made to trot, or a company of brave infantrymen to march in step.

Many diverse, ingenious toys were invented. They included the pecking hens and a woodpecker tapping insistently at a tree trunk. The greatest favourite with the children, though, was a carriage or sleigh drawn by a trotting horse, with a coachman up in front.

As the toy industry broadened in scope, so did the skill of the master carvers grow. From the animated "Blacksmiths" and scissor-movement group, they turned to the depiction of a shepherd boy playing his pipe, a tipsy muzhik fumbling at a concertina, and, finally, the silly barinya. So what was originally an innocuous child's toy unnoticeably developed into a barb of satire.

With rising mastery came the multifigure group. It was only natural for the craftsman to try to produce in wood all that was familiar, such as scenes from peasant life or the content of folk tales. Among the host of themes used were, for example, cabbage-chopping, ploughing, flax-threshing, tea-drinking and popular festivities. Then the element of animation was introduced into this sculptural group or "menage" as well. Hung by a thread, the simplest of plummets caused the arms to move up and down, while tree leaves, attached by the slenderest of spirals, quivered at the slightest jolt.

Russian carving enjoyed great success abroad. German, French and American buyers were attracted both by the craftsmen's virtuosity and the exoticism of vast and enigmatic Russia.

Paradoxically enough, the keener the interest, the less was the carver rewarded for his skill. According to a long-standing custom, the peasant craftsmen sold their work to a middleman jobber, who naturally sought as big a profit as possible. "The boundary-carved and ravine-pitted land . . . deteriorated with every year," a contemporary observed. "Meanwhile, Sergievsky wholesalers

Scissor-movement toy, 1913. By V. Poninov

tightened the screw. On religious holidays a more or less decent price was paid, but out of season carvings went for a song." A skilled carver had to slave some 15 or 16 hours a day to earn enough to keep body and soul together.

In vain, however, did the peasant craftsman try to compete with the increasing influx of factory-made toys. The more wooden figures he made, the less thought he gave to quality and artistic merit. His craft had become nothing but back-breaking toil and was no longer cause for aesthetic delight.

Reminiscences

DIGGING into one's recollections, one always looks for a landmark, perhaps a letter, note or article, a building, street or even whole town, to resurrect in detail a day, month or year long past. It thus happened that a very recently created artistic object threw into bold relief a picture of life 70 years earlier.

One day a Soviet museum curator asked the wood carvers of Bogorodskoye to carve a picture of village life in the old days. They agreed, each secretly hoping to be entrusted with this honourable task. However, at a general meeting, they decided to assign the work to their doyen, Fyodor Balayev.

 One month later his piece, bearing the rather unusual name of "Father's Legacy", was ready.

It showed a weary peasant woman scattering handfuls of grain from her basket, as she slowly trudged across a field. Behind her a spavined nag, nuzzling her back, pulled at a set of harrows. A barefoot, tousle-headed boy plodded along by her side.

Old-timers among the curious neighbours who came to see the carving, noticed that the sower bore a surprising resemblance to Balayev's dead mother. This was a scene remembered from childhood.

Balayev's father died in 1889, when the boy was but 12 years old. All his widowed mother and he inherited were a decrepit horse, a set of knives and chisels and, the main treasure, the secret of how to transform dead limewood into figures of people, birds and beasts, that seemed alive.

Fyodor grew up a skilled craftsman. He was taken to the Russian National Fair in St. Petersburg as a living exhibit. There he spent a whole fortnight carving for hours on end. He modelled roosters, horses, cows, hens and shepherds. And all the time a well-dressed crowd of idlers looked on, exclaiming in a mixture of Russian and foreign tongues: "Oh, how lovely! How talented!" The sated, bored metropolitan public derived vast entertainment, watching this illiterate peasant who showed such great talent.

On closing day a staid, portly courtier in a gold-laced uniform presented Balayev with a certificate of honour, a medal and imperial consent to the establishment of a carvers' co-operative in Bogorodskoye. Fyodor returned home without a farthing in his pocket. The money needed to set the co-operative going was not forthcoming.

However, though the tsar had given his blessing, Volchkov was against it. The tsar ruled all of Russia; Volchkov meanwhile owned only the biggest house of all in Bogorodskoye. But Volchkov was on the spot, while the tsar was far away. In Bogorodskoye he wielded more influence than the tsar.

The tsar believed a co-operative profitable, thinking it would net more in tax receipts from the peasantry. For Volchkov, however, the co-operative

"Tops and Roots." A fairy-tale scene, 1945. By I. Stulov ▶

"Bear Playing the Bass Fiddle", 1953. By M. Barinov

"Singing Bear." By M. Barinov ►

meant a financial loss. He was a wholesaler, a jobber. He paid the peasant craftsmen in shop-soiled products and shoddy calico reselling their handiwork at fairs and in the cities at a fabulous profit.

For the craftsmen the co-operative meant relief from the arbitrary despotism of the wholesaler. Together with Fyodor Balayev, newly returned from St. Petersburg, Bogorodskoye's ace carvers Andrei Chushkin, Leonty Zinin, and Filipp Yeroshkin, resolved to mortgage their belongings to raise the necessary funds. They elected Andrei Chushkin, for whom they had the greatest respect, their elder, and decided to accept as members only the best of the best. All desirous of joining had to show their work and pass a special test.

They received much assistance from the artist N. Bartram, a connoisseur of the Russian wooden toy, who helped the carvers of Bogorodskoye to start new lines, and got them contracts.

The co-operative made good progress. By the beginning of the First World War, it was manufacturing some 150 different kinds of toys and sculptural miniatures.

In October 1917 the Revolution broke out. The country was seething like a bubbling cauldron. The old order tumbled down; but to build a new life the Civil War first had to be won.

In Bogorodskoye, too, there were changes. Some carvers joined the army, others deserted their craft for farming. The co-operative came to a standstill.

After the Civil War ended, and the rifle and hand grenade gave way to spade and pick, life reverted slowly but surely to a peaceful tenor. The working folk, who were now masters of the country, were poor and could not as yet afford costly china, glassware or carved bone work. The only adornment in reach of every pocket was the wooden miniature.

The new customer, the working man, naturally desired new objects that accorded with his aesthetic ideals. This was something the carvers could not adapt themselves to at once. After all it is always hard for an adult to forswear immediately an ingrained habit. This is a process which takes years.

Several craftsmen tried their hand at figures of Red Armymen and working women. However, these pieces continued to resemble the old familiar hussars and barinyas and were not what was wanted. The carvers of Bogorodskoye had to blaze new trails.

Whenever Fyodor Balayev recollects that period, he steals a glance, as he smooths his bushy whiskers, at the corner where the small time-darkened bust of an old man stands silent witness to his creative searchings.

One day, at the close of the 1920s, Fyodor Balayev happened to see at his friend's home in Zagorsk the china figure of a bearded old man with an amazingly clever face.

"Who's that?" he wondered.

"That's the writer Lev Tolstoi," he was told. "He was a count, but he stuck up for the common people."

Balayev had never read Tolstoi, let alone seen him; but he couldn't forget about the writer's having "stuck up for the common people", and back home he whittled a portrait of Tolstoi.

Portraiture was a novelty for the Bogorodskoye carver. However, the obligation to copy out the likeness cramped initiative and turned the joy of creative work into monotonous drudgery. Nor did it delight the buyer. This was because instead of a sculpture on a modern theme or the image of an animal possessing a comical, almost human grimace, he was offered the wooden replica of a good china statuette.

Again the carvers of Bogorodskoye had to hunt for new forms. In Fyodor Balayev's home are five limewood bas-reliefs of a street vendor, a hunter, and janitor, revealing a technique many sculptors might well envy. However, the members of the co-operative were not appreciative.

"How can one know what they are when they have no backs?" one of the carvers let drop.

The Bogorodskoye tradition of dimensional carving derives from a centuries-old blend of the finest and pithiest aspects of the handiwork of many generations. A violation of this glorious tradition spelt retrogression.

Lack of experience caused the young talented sculptor P. Balandin to overlook that point. In the mid-thirties he gave the co-operative some new animal prototypes—a lion, hippopotamus, rhinoceros, camel, zebra, antelope, and monkey. Balandin thought these small figures would look well against light-toned wallpaper on a shelf in the room of a factory worker or office clerk. Giving his imagination free rein, he forgot the customary Bogorodskoye tradition of imparting familiar, human traits to animal miniatures. Since Balandin's beasts had no live characteristics, they served merely as a decorative ornament. No wonder that after a few sets of this new menagerie had been produced, the carvers consigned it to oblivion.

The early thirties witnessed the almost simultaneous appearance of "A Collective Farm Meeting" by Fyodor Yeroshkin, "The Civil War Girl Guerrilla" and "Blast Furnace Man" by Ivan Stulov and "The Chapayev Machine-Gun Carriage", the last being the collective effort of a group of students of the Bogorodskoye school of carving.

The craftsmen sought to reflect the new life that was in the making. Though their efforts were far from perfect, the subject-matter taken furnished the only correct answer to their long, agonising quest.

In the mid-thirties Bogorodskoye craftsmen produced dozens of carvings on modern themes that were perfect in form, composition and execution—largely due to a revival of past experience.

Fyodor Balayev's "Chelyuskin Crew" group serves as a reminder of this process.

The 60-year-old craftsman took the heroism of the intrepid Soviet Arctic explorers as a symbol of the Soviet man's new moral fibre. A radio broadcast about the brave deeds of the Chelyuskin crew induced him to reflect this glorious feat in wood, but for a long time he could not find the right approach.

 Nearly two years passed. All thought the craftsman had abandoned the idea, when one fine day, Fyodor sent his boys to the library for every book about the Chelyuskin and its crew they could lay their hands on.

The two boys in turn read aloud magazines, booklets and time-faded newspapers to the carver, who sipped cups of tea that grew lukewarm as he avidly listened to every word.

Work got under way. One after another Balayev stored away the carved figures of men, polar bears, and huskies. Winter crept up almost unnoticeably. Bogorodskoye, built on a tall hill, was hemmed in by snow-blanketed fields. As soon as dawn broke, the carver donned his sheepskin and pulling up the collar, struck out into the fields to see the snowdrifts.

By spring his task was finished. The several groups of miniatures were not mounted on the usual board. All they shared in common was the story of the Chelyuskin tragedy, and the rescue. Since the figures are independent they may be transposed at will without fear of breaking up the general idea.

This solution was no novelty for the master carvers of Bogorodskoye. It had been known before the Revolution. Balayev had merely revived a forgotten method.

Soon Balayev's elder son, Alexander, emulating his father's example, put a multifigure composition called "The Durov Railway" before the co-operative's art council.

This piece shows a tiny wooden locomotive pulling a string of cars along rails consisting of narrow strips of wood. A stupid duck, seated on a station bench, phlegmatically awaits the arrival of the train. The train conductor, a fox, licks its chops, staring hard at the would-be passenger. Meanwhile a deeply preoccupied porter bear hastily lumbers by.

Other talented carvers, notably N. Yeroshkin, V. Polinov, G. Shishkin and I. Volchkov borrowed Fyodor Balayev's method or rather his idea of reviving the artifices of their forefathers. A particularly happy carving was Ivan Volchkov's "Lumberjacks". Disposed amidst a goodly number of trees, that follow the old tradition in execution, are figures of young men and women holding saws and axes. Also introduced are stacks of logs and felled, but still not stripped, trunks.

Meanwhile, Yeroshkin, Polinov and Shishkin resolved to revive still older methods. Widely current among Bogorodskoye carvers at the close of the past century were the so-called "menages", which were genre scenes from peasant life having all the figures mounted on one board. The carvers linked several of these groups, giving different separate episodes, into a whole story in wood. Diverse scenes of modern village life were followed by whole puppet shows for children. These toys, which were not animated, but which provided several episodes, included "Masha and the Bear-Cubs", "Once an Old Lady Had a Grey Kid" and "The Sun, the Moon and Voron Voronovich, the Raven".

By wedding novel solutions to the best of past traditions, Bogorodskoye master carvers progressed with seven league strides, marking their road of advance with such milestones as letters of commendation, and medals and certificates won at exhibitions and fairs both in the USSR and abroad.

ogorodskoye Today

ONE can gain an idea of what Bogorodskoye is like today, without even going outside Moscow. Suffice it to take a short stroll through the streets, notably Stanislavsky Street, preferably during the winter or spring school holidays.

Why at that particular time? Because when schools are empty and children throng the theatres, cinemas and clubs, the Folk Arts and Handicrafts Museum in the old mansion on Stanislavsky Street bills special displays.

ear Photographing the on." By M. Barash-. Reflection of modern elopments in Bogorod-ye carving

At small tables placed in the huge room next to show cases exhibiting diverse specimens of folk art, deft master carvers in wood and bone, lacemakers, and jewellers ply their craft, to provide school pupils with a graphic demonstration of the entire creative process.

The crowd is usually thickest around the table where small blocks of wood are transformed into comical miniature figures. That gifted craftsman Mikhail Barinov, who has been working for several years now at the Bogorodskoye Factory—the art co-operative was reorganised into a factory in 1960—picks up a small prism-shaped plank with his left hand and takes a sharp knife in his right. In 10 to 15 minutes there appear before enchanted eyes a whole row of figures: a bearded janitor holding a broom, a smug, pot-bellied bureaucrat carrying a bulging briefcase, and an underground railway stationmaster.

Let us now leave the museum, with the craftsmen amidst the throngs of inquisitive school children, and continue on our way. We may choose at random any of the gift shops, because all are sure to have several show cases or shelves displaying contemporary Bogorodskoye woodwork.

A closer look discloses the familiar janitor, bureaucrat or stationmaster. Nowadays these are painted. The stationmaster is in a black coat and red cap. The bureaucrat wears a grey fedora, and a black suit, and carries a russet-brown briefcase. These $1^{1}/_{2}$-inch painted figures come from Bogorodskoye.

They first saw the light of day in 1957, when the USSR was getting ready for the Sixth World Youth and Student Festival, and everyone sought to delight the guests from abroad with some novelty. The master carvers of Bogorodskoye offered several small, cheap souvenirs that would easily fit into the pocket of a departing foreigner. They turned out specially for the Festival 15 small figures in folk costumes: one for each Union Republic. The following year they produced more, now in a different vein. Some were funny, some satirical, such as the bureaucrat or the ultra-fashionable Miss.

At the shop we visit we shall find next to these miniatures such old acquaintances as the "Blacksmiths", the pecking hens, an animated group of skiers or a collective-farm herd. There are not many of these toys, however, and they are modestly tucked away in a corner, yielding pride of place to modern novelties No wonder since the "Blacksmiths" appeared at a time when the craftsmen had not the slightest inkling of the telephone, bicycle or camera. Today a bear-cub chatting over the telephone, a hare taking a photograph,

or a bruin on a tricycle, are run-of-the-mill Bogorodskoye products, executed, however, in the same traditional centuries-old manner.

Today even these toys have had to step down to give way to such pieces as a bear staring agape at a model of the globe with a sputnik whizzing around it, or a bear launching a rocket.

During the last war the carvers produced some fine pieces. I. Stulov gave an excellent presentation of Soviet women in those grim years, with his figures of the girl partisan, the girl blast-furnace operator, the hospital nurse and the collective-farm woman. A. Pronin produced a toy showing a bearded partisan herding into captivity at bayonet point a nazi soldier shod in a semblance of the plaited bast footwear that the peasant wore before the Revolution. By pressing a catch, one causes the partisan to prick the nazi's posterior. The toy-maker's son, M. Pronin, elaborated upon the subject, carving a large group called "Partisans Bivouacking in the Forest". It shows partisans resting after a battle. Their rifles are stacked in pyramids, a fire is burning, and outside the tents, pitched among the trees, men clean their weapons or read books.

Other sculptural pieces that the craftsman produced in that period included "Ivan Susanin", "The Russian Heroes", "Alexander Nevsky" and "The Soviet Fighting Man and Liberator".

Many Bogorodskoye carvers were killed in the war. Some of the survivors came back only for a look at their native village and then sought employment at

"Heron." Of limewood. By I. Stulov

52 construction jobs and factories elsewhere. However, most were only too eager to resume their favourite craft.

In Mikhail Barashkov's case, though, demobilisation was but the first stepping-stone to a new career.

He had volunteered for the front straight from school. With his gun crew he marched hundreds of miles across Russia. One battle he took part in was that for the liberation of the ancient Russian town of Novgorod.

After the city was taken, the gun crew now billeted in a small cottage busied themselves with personal matters; one wrote a letter home, another repaired his greatcoat, and a third cleaned his tommy-gun. Perched on the doorstep Mikhail drew forth a knife from the top of his jackboot and proceeded to carve the figure of a soldier from a stick. He had developed the habit of tallying battle scores in this fashion. A soldier meant that his gun had wiped out an enemy platoon, a cottage, that an enemy gun emplacement had been destroyed, while a tank naturally implied that one of these monsters had been put out of action. The mistress of the house approached the sergeant, curious to see what he was doing.

"You've certainly got a gift for working in wood," she observed. "It's not everybody as has it. Did you ever hear about our Novgorod craftsmen? There was one old man who lived in Novgorod. Palitsyn was the name. He used to carve wooden figures of people. The neighbours say some of his things were even shown in a museum in Leningrad itself. When the nazis came, almost the first thing they did was to go over to his place. He wasn't able to evacuate, you see. So the swine tell him: 'We want to send your things off to Germany.' To that Palitsyn says: 'All right. You come along tomorrow. I'll have everything ready by then.'

"When they came next morning, the old master was breaking up the last charred bits with his poker. He had burnt everything, had destroyed everything he had ever made. So they shot him, and then said he'd had contacts with the partisans and had helped them, which he probably did."

Much water has flowed under the bridges since. Back in Bogorodskoye, the first thing Mikhail did was to go straight to the factory. Life was not life for him without the fragrant aroma of freshly sawn blocks of wood and a set of chisels. His neighbour was a young craftsman freshly out of the carving school. There were many things Mikhail had to learn from scratch. However, the demobbed sergeant was persistent.

The years sped by. Today Mikhail Barashkov feels perfectly at home in the newly-built spacious workroom. Now and again, he will sit down to admire the handiwork of some younger talented craftsman. Or he might give helpful advice.

"Now look here," he may say to a young carver, "you've got the arms a bit too short."

Stopping at another bench he will exclaim: "Now look at that bear of yours! He's all doubled up in pain, not singing happily. Mikhail Barinov, the artist who created that bear, took great pains with it. First he studied the people around and only then did he take up the knife. Now when you young folks go around singing in the evening, do you look like that? So please get it right." And on he will go.

Wooden toys by Vadim Strakhov

 Barashkov scrutinises the finished article with a very carping eye. Though the woodwork goes through the procedure of inspection and is examined by the chief artist, the craftsman prefers to rely on his own judgement. He has just deposited on the shelf several carved figures of the characters populating the Russian folk tale "Tops and Roots". The peasant's smooth smock, the large mesh of the wicker basket, and the wavy lines of the bear's shaggy coat introduce a very colourful note to this extremely integral, composite piece.

The "Tops and Roots" figures stand next to completed miniatures of Tsar Dodon, a character from Pushkin's *Golden Cockerel.* He is accepting the Golden Cockerel from the astrologer. These pieces will definitely get a top rating. They were carved by the experienced craftsman Nikolai Levin, from the prototypes created by I. Stulov. Levin has been working at the factory for thirty years now and the most responsible assignments are always entrusted to him.

Today, though, Barashkov is most particular, even with regard to Levin. That is because very soon these figures will be packed in crates with many others such as "Sadko Plucking the Dulcimer", "The Bear Bending the Yoke", "The Singing Bear" and "Orlov Trotter" and be shipped abroad to Brussels, Paris, London and New York, where people will gaze in wonder at the handiwork of folk craftsmen from the faraway Russian village of Bogorodskoye.

Though this hamlet is some distance from the nearest railway, and three miles of thick aspen woods separate it from a highway, the radio and huge television aerials topping each roof with its fanciful drapery of lacelike carving, show clearly that life nowadays in this once backwoods village is quite in step with the times.

ine logs crackled gaily. The flames cleaved the darkness, and a profusion of sparks floated down to the riverside.

A troop of the Streltsi Guard mounted the night watch. Though mess time was long over, no one thought of moving away from the comforting glow of the fire.

"Uncle Klim!" blond Vanya Fedotov broke the silence, "I see you've just finished your fearful lions. How did you acquire that skill? Did you learn it as a boy or did the good God grant it you?"

"Look at the fellow," another soldier intervened. "He wants to know whether it was God or not. Tomorrow the verger will twist out all that curiosity of yours by the ear."

"Come, come, Arseny! Let the lad understand what's what. Why, he might become a pretty good craftsman himself one day. Now you just listen, Vanya, and remember what I say.

"Father and I were freemen, craftsmen," uncle Klim began. "Father wielded an axe all his life. As a boy I was very fond of painting flowers on the walls and doors with clay, chalk and even a charred piece of wood. When I grew a little older, I tried my hand at carving. I liked the result and had another go at it. The second time was still better. I amused myself carving for quite a while. When I became still older I joined a team of craftsmen working on a house for Prince Kurakin.

"That changed my whole life. When I saw the serving girl Annie I knew love had come. A bit later I found out she had a fancy for me too. I wondered how to get the Prince to agree to us marrying.

"Now though I was racking my brains, the Prince was craftier. He didn't object to our getting married. He even sent us some wedding presents. But after the wedding he refused to let her go and kept her in the scullery.

THE EIGHTH WONDER OF THE WORLD

"A whole year went like that. When the house was done and we had carved woodware galore, the Prince bound us over to Patriarch Nikon himself. It seems his Beatitude needed craftsmen badly. Well, I did my best to make the carving as fanciful as I could, so that Annie would stay in his good graces. In this manner eleven years went by, until Boyar Khitrovo requisitioned us for the Armoury.

"However, it's time to turn in. The clerks were prattling today that the Boyar himself will come tomorrow."

Boyar Khitrovo supervised the tsar's Armoury, centre of Russian arts and handicrafts in the seventeenth century. He requisitioned for his workshops the best armourers, jewellers, wood and ivory carvers, painters and potters from all over Russia. It was in the chambers hard by the Kremlin's Borovitsky Gates that they created their exquisite handiwork.

When in 1667 Tsar Alexei Mikhailovich bade these ingenious craftsmen to construct a new imperial palace they were not at all daunted. Some six centuries earlier the palace of the Prince of Kiev had evoked the admiration of travellers. Amidst the dense northern forests the sharp spires of wooden churches pierced the heavens. The banks of the Oka and the Volga were studded with peasant cottages ornamented with magnificent carving. Now, however, the plan was to erect an edifice of unsurpassed beauty in the village of Kolomenskoye.

The Tsar sought by sumptuous extravagance to emphasise Russia's grandeur and might. The new Kolomenskoye Palace was to be such a token of imperial splendour.

For two whole years old Arseny, Klim Mikhailov, his apprentice Vanya Fedotov and hundreds of other master craftsmen toiled away unflaggingly through winter cold, autumn rain and summer heat.

A whole ensemble of fairy-tale grace, a tall many-storied palace that was a township in itself, arose amidst thickets of slender birch-trees on a bend in the Moskva River. Ethereal galleries and roofed passageways linked the separate structures into one composite whole. Tower spires alternated with heart-shaped and barrel-like rooftops. Elaborate open-worked eaves overhung fat

◄ *Kolomenskoye Palace, a wonder in wood*

carved pillars. At entrances ruddy-brown lions yawned ferociously while exotic birds fanned their luxuriant plumage on either side of the numerous windows. On sunny days, the gaily painted ornamentation flaunted every colour of the rainbow. Indeed, a wonderland—made entirely of wood!

The ancients had known seven wonders of the world. These were the Pyramids, the Colossus of Rhodes, the Statue of Zeus by Phidias, the Mausoleum at Halicarnassus, the Temple of Diana at Ephesus, the Hanging Gardens of Babylon, and the Pharos of Alexandria. Now the Tsar of all Russia displayed the eighth wonder, the handiwork of serf craftsmen.

"The ancients knew of seven wonders. The eighth, this palace, is of our time," the celebrated seventeenth-century author Semyon Polotsky remarked of the Kolomenskoye Palace.

This edifice which Russian carpenters, joiners and carvers put up in the space of two years, elicited enthusiastic admiration from foreigners. Thus, one Reitenfels observed in 1671 that "it is so marvellously adorned with carved work and gilt that one could take it for a toy newly out of its box".

The Tsar in his "munificent benevolence" did not forget the real creators of this marvel. "On this day, the thirtieth of May," the clerk chanted to the crowd of artisans, "His Majesty has deigned to bestow upon the master carvers Arseny, Klim Mikhailov, David Pavlov, Andrei Ivanov and Gerasim Akulov and their apprentices Yevstignei Semyonov, Dmitry Sidorov, Ivan Fedotov and Kuzma Yevseyev a length of Hamburg cloth each."

The clerk had long waddled off the porch but the artisans still stood rooted to the spot scarcely able to believe their ears. They vainly hoped there might have been something they had misheard or missed. Was this measly length of cloth all there was to the Tsar's benevolence?

Dragoons rode up and dispersed the crowd.

"What are you gaping at?" Mikhailov gruffly shouted at his apprentice.

"Well Uncle Klim, I think I've understood a thing or two this day."

"A thing or two you say? Well, that's good! In a year or two, let's hope you'll be a very understanding craftsman indeed."

We shall probably never know Ivan Fedotov's lot. He may have built a palace for Prince Golitsyn or for the Grand Prince Romodanovsky, or he may have fled from the tender mercies of the Tsar and the Boyars and taken refuge with the free Cossacks along the Don.

Parquetry at the Ostankino palace

 As the decades rolled by, that great carved toy, the Palace of Kolomenskoye, fell into disuse. In 1767, exactly one hundred years after it was built, Catherine the Great ordered it to be demolished.

But the creative urge of the folk carvers could not be killed. The beams and planks of the dismantled Kolomenskoye Palace were still rotting, when at the other end of Moscow caravans of peasant carts, piled high with beams, converged on the village of Ostankino, where Count Sheremetyev had conceived the whim of building a wooden country villa. Serf architects, artists, carvers, and cabinet-makers toiled to produce another masterpiece.

"Our bonded artisans," the steward of Ostankino Agapov reported to his master the Count, "are working with all conceivable speed, idling neither on holidays nor Sundays, and toiling by candle light even from four o'clock in the morning till ten o'clock at night. And to expedite their labours," he added, "a hussar, not of their parts, has been detailed to supervise them."

The palace was finished by the spring of 1798.

Carved table legs

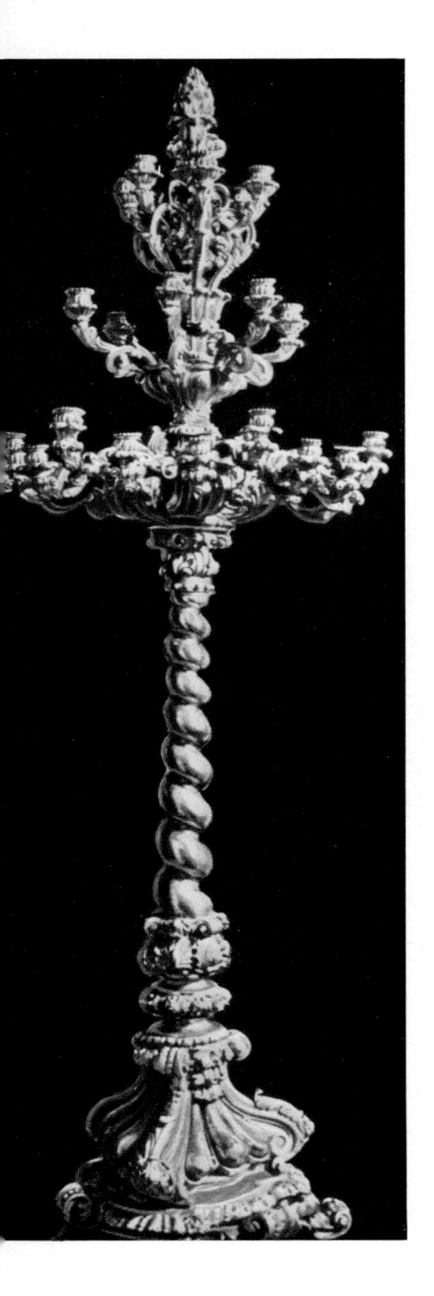

The seven wonders of the ancients were made of marble, granite, fired clay, ivory, bronze and gold. The Russian serf artisans wrought their wonders from wood and in incredibly difficult conditions. Oak, lime, birch, and nut served them in place of stone and metal.

Columns carved from whole tree trunks were plastered and painted to resemble marble. The huge vases, sphinxes and chandeliers were all of wood, finely coated with gold or bronze. Carved work underlay the entire ornamentation. Gilded, it framed entrances, doorways and windows. Ballroom walls were inset with enormous carved wooden panels. The intricately cut garlands of flowers, the figures of people and animals and the scroll work adorning the furniture, frames, and candelabra evoke mixed feelings of amazement and admiration. It is indeed hard to believe that these exquisite petals of roses in full bloom, the ears of grain, cornflowers and daisies, coiled snakes, defiant lions and mountain sheep are all made of wood by calloused hands unable even to pen the names of their owners.

In the court diary of Stanislaw Poniatowski, King of Poland, is an entry describing his visit to the Palace of Ostankino: "As for the carpentry, gilt work, mirrors, window and door frames, and the parquet, all was of superb execution, without a single blemish. Of the several hundred craftsmen and artists that worked there, no more than four or five were foreigners. The remainder were not just Russians; nearly all were Count Sheremetyev's serfs. Without confirmation this would indeed arouse incredulity, so elegantly is everything wrought. Indeed, His Majesty had scarcely ever seen a more eminently suitable place for grand and solemn festivity."

Chandelier carved entirely of wood

Mosaic parquetry

The names of the master carvers remained unknown for some 120 years. Only after 1917, when scholars were able to peruse Count Sheremetyev's personal archives, were several names discovered in the steward's accounts and the Count's own letters.

In May 1796 there was an entry that "because of a headache, carver Ivan Mochalin has failed to report for work the third day now". In September of the same year, Sheremetyev ordered several serving boys to be apprenticed to carver Ivan Mochalin.

Designated in a payroll dated 1802 under No. 659 and following a list of domestics is the name of carver Ivan Mazokhin. Another two names unearthed are Fyodor Nikiforov and Gavrila Nemkov.

Today the names of these serf craftsmen are inscribed in marble in the palace lobby. Since the advent of Soviet power millions have visited the museum of serf art at Ostankino. All were amazed by the genius of the master carvers of Ostankino. Before leaving, many a visitor would check his steps at the memorial plaque to jot down the names of men who had made these marvels. Some may have very well been distant relatives of the carvers, or future celebrities who, in their own right, will become the subject of monographs or stories about craftsmen that will some day be written.

WOODEN GOLD

From Volga Forests

ir John was as pleased as Punch. That morning his three-master had docked in London with a large consignment of Russian hemp and building timber from Archangel. Not this had put him in such good humour though. Hemp and timber were ordinary enough; his ships had plied between London and the distant northern city for many a year now. The Englishman was happy because of a gift from his sailing master—a large chest containing the gilt woodenware which only the people of distant Muscovy could make.

At the banquet next day Sir John was sure his cronies would be amazed when they saw the platters, spoons, and bowls decorated with such fantastic flowers. The merchant rubbed his hands with glee as he imagined one of his friends picking up a gleaming seemingly massive bowl and putting it down, wonderstruck on finding that it had been carved of wood.

"Did you learn the name of the craftsman who made this?" the merchant asked the captain of the vessel.

"I made inquiries, sir," came the reply. "The Muscovites give a truly odd name, sir. They said it was Kho-khlo-ma."

Had Sir John had the opportunity of looking at a map of Russia published in 1614, some fifty years earlier, he may have noticed in the middle of a green area, denoting forests, northeast of Nizhni-Novgorod, a tiny tower with the legend Khokhloma underneath it. On Sundays the square at the foot of the wall of this small fortress became a market where amid sacks of rye and oats peasant craftsmen from villages in the vicinity traded their painted woodenware. In this way the fortress came to lend its name to the glistening bowls and spoons. Mention of Khokhloma is first found in chronicles dating back to the mid-sixteenth century, to the reign of Ivan the Terrible.

In 1618 Tsar Mikhail Romanov presented Khokhloma and the

 neighbouring villages—in what are now the Konvernino and Semyonov districts of Gorky Region—to the court clerk Ivan Gramotin. Some fifteen years later, the latter in turn bequeathed Khokhloma to the Troitse-Sergievsky Monastery.

Volga woodsmen had long been famed for their skill in the making of woodenware, of which token is found in the chronicles for 1439 that were penned by the scribes of St. Makarius' Monastery on the Volga. For Russia woodenware is no exotic curio. Throughout the ages, in both town and country, people ate porridge and soup with wooden spoons from wooden bowls and platters and drank kvass (a traditional Russian beverage fermented from black bread and malt) from carved ladles and loving cups. Khokhloma ware must have indeed been remarkable for the chronicler to have mentioned it.

Let us refer to the chronicles of another religious establishment the Troitse-Sergievsky Monastery, which was overlord of Khokhloma. In an inventory conducted in 1642, the monastery treasurer reported among other articles 9,570 loving cups and 17,000 wooden spoons painted in cinnabar and red lead. Khokhloma craftsmen were conspicuous among makers of woodenware for the handsomely decorated products.

The craftsman would use a fine pointed brush to paint on the bottom of a wooden bowl a circle radiating sinuous lines, which, climbing over the rim, decorated the outer wall as well. The pattern was reminiscent of a child's drawing of the sun and, incidentally, was known in popular idiom as "the redhead"—a name given to the sun since time immemorial.

Then one day a craftsman introduced the square, which he called the "gingerbread". Later the square was transformed into a lozenge.

With time the craftsmen grew tired of these motifs, and attempted to depict the beauties of nature. So did the "readhead" and lozenge gradually yield to a lush floral pattern.

By this time craftsmen had also learned to make the paintwork fast. For the paint to lie evenly on the roughish surface, the spoon had first to be very thinly coated with a special loam. Then it was bathed in linseed oil to cause the paint to adhere. The painted spoon was given several coatings of a varnish made of flaxseed oil and then oven-dried. It emerged smooth and glistening, proof against piping hot cabbage soup and steaming porridge.

Only the poor ate from woodenware. In the palaces food was served on silver and pewter. So the following episode may very well have taken place.

One day a rich man presented a peasant craftsman with a pewter platter. Since it looked an ugly duckling among its gay handsome wooden brethren, the craftsman decided to paint it in the same fashion as he painted his wooden utensils. He cleansed the surface, painted it, varnished it and put it into the oven to dry. When he took it out, he gaped with wonder and summoned all his neighbours to witness the miracle. He had put in pewter but had taken out gold. It was the same platter and the same plant motif, but conspicuous now against a golden background. Indeed a plate fit for the tsar himself. The reason was simple—the heat of the oven had caused the varnish to yellow, and through it the pewter gleamed golden.

The craftsman then essayed the same device using a wooden platter. After bathing it in linseed oil, he rubbed it over with powdered tin. The ultimate result seemed heavy and massive as if made of the finest gold. This was ware of wooden gold, never seen before.

The story of its birth may have been quite different, though, because, after all said and done, Russian icon painters had long known how to give their paintings a golden background.

Soon not only the people from nearby villages, but also shrewd merchants from distant parts and even from overseas flocked to the Makariev Fair, the

Old painted wooden bowl with traditional Khokhloma floral motif

grandest on the Volga, to purchase this ware, not piece by piece, but by weight, by the pood and ton.

However, the more the craftsman sold, the more in tithes and tributes did he have to forfeit to his feudal overlord, whether the Troitse-Sergievsky Monastery, or Count Sheremetyev, that same nobleman who commanded the exquisite wooden palace to be built at Ostankino.

Still bigger vampires were the merchants from the towns of Semyonov and Nizhni-Novgorod hard by. No wonder the Volga woodsmen paraphrased the old saying "from the frying pan into the fire" to run "from the priests to the merchants". The latter fixed their own prices and had the craftsmen, who sank deeper into debt, completely under their thumbs.

While the artisans slaved away fifteen hours a day, sturdy two-storey mansions and squat storehouses mushroomed in Semyonov. In 1797 the city mayor reported that the population carried on no farming at all. He then listed all the painted woodenware that had been sold at the Makariev Fair in the space of a year, including 500,000 bowls, 300,000 platters, 100,000 cups and 800,000 spoons.

Still extant are the spoon pattern names "puff-ball" and "face". The cheapest type of spoon was decorated with a pattern consisting of tiny, symmetrically disposed stars, impressed by means of a stamp made from the skin of a puff-ball; hence its name. The craftsman was obliged to enliven a hundred out of every thousand spoons thus made with an additional decoration of small red flowers. The jobber, who paid a uniform price for the entire thousand, would put the "puff-ball" spoons at the bottom beneath the painted ones, and sell the entire basket wholesale for quite a price, claiming that all the spoons were the same as those on the top, which he displayed at "face" value. Hence the second name.

Gilded Khokhloma woodenware sold well far outside Russia too and the jobbers waxed rich.

However, this trade did not flourish long. A formidable rival appeared in the shape of the cheap and handy factory-made china and glass which, in the second half of the nineteenth century, completely ousted Khokhloma ware. Whole families flocked to the towns in search of a livelihood. Rapidly diminishing quantities of painted woodenware were offered for sale at fairs, and little by little craftsmanship deteriorated.

First to sound the alarm was the Governor and his staff. However, the demand to revive the craft derived not from a love for the folk arts, but from

Modern Khokhloma ware with traditional ornamental motifs

the drastically diminishing tax returns. It was decided that the Khokhloma trade must be re-established at all costs.

In the 1880s a craze for "everything Russian" infected the Russian bourgeoisie. Pandering to their tastes many architects and artists endeavoured in their work to blend individual elements of ancient Russian folk art with the massive vulgarity of merchant luxury. Thus, in architecture, a peculiar style that was subsequently sarcastically dubbed the "cockerel fashion" became the rage. At any rate, the artist Durnovo, whom the Nizhni-Novgorod Zemstvo (district assembly) had specially invited to revive the craft, resolved to turn this situation to advantage.

He started with the manufacture of painted furniture, suggesting a new pattern that was a modernised ornament of the interlace culled from ancient manuscripts. However, as it had lost its erstwhile elegance and beauty, it smacked more of a tangle of crude belts, and was very aptly dubbed "tripe" by the village craftsmen.

To produce this unfamiliar and incomprehensible pattern faster and better, the craftsman devised a method whereby the ornament was very rapidly and accurately reproduced on wood by pricking it out with a needle from the paper pattern. This "speed-up" killed creative imagination but pleased the jobbers. Thus there appeared at fairs and in shops massive, cumbersome "à la Russe" cupboards, beds, tables, armchairs and stools.

Now though it is possible to dictate to a jobbing worker whose goal is easy money, it is not so simple to kill the aesthetic taste of a real artist wishing to continue the creative tradition of generations. However hard Durnovo sought to implant alien motifs, he was powerless when faced with real talent. Some craftsmen, such as Fyodor Krasilnikov, Stepan Yuzikov and the Podogov brothers, followed the old traditions. Their tables and chairs were exquisitely decorated with a cunningly contrived ornament of gay flowers presented against a background of black and gold. At the Russian National Exhibition in 1913, Fyodor Krasilnikov earned a Medal of Honour, which, however, did nothing to ease his lot. He continued to decorate furniture for the grasping jobber Kudryashov for a miserable pittance.

Nor did other craftsmen fare any better. Still current is the legend of the bedroom suite with which the Podogov brothers attempted to outwit Krasilnikov. Since they were well aware of the difficulties of competing with this talented craftsman in creating a new ornamental motif, they decided to go one better in technique, turning out a dressing-table with a wooden mirror. So deftly did they coat the wood, that after the oven drying it indeed shone like a mirror, but with a golden tint. It is further claimed that the merchant Malyshev sold this wooden mirror in Germany for a large sum, which he spent on acquiring a plate of real gold for a wedding present for his daughter. The Podogovs at any rate continued to eat off wood.

In his brilliant work, *The Development of Capitalism in Russia,* Lenin provides, in the chapter dealing with the capitalist manufactory in Russian industry, a comprehensive picture of the dire plight of the craftsmen at the end of the 19th century, and incontrovertibly demonstrates that every handicraft and artisan was absolutely dependent on the capitalist.

“The celebrated wood-spoon industry of the Semyonov Uyezd, Nizhni-Novgorod Gubernia,” Lenin wrote, “is close to capitalist manufacture in organisation. True, there are no big workshops . . . but we find deeply-rooted division of labour and the complete subjection of the mass of part-job workers to capital. Before it is ready, the spoon passes through no less than 10 hands, the buyers-up getting some of the operations done by specially hired workers (for example, for varnishing); some of the villages specialise in particular operations.” Quoting further from a statistical handbook put out by the provincial zemstvo, Lenin went on to note that “it is all the same to the spoon-makers whether they work for hire at the master’s cost and on his premises, or are

On the bottom of the bowl—Khokhloma “gingerbread” pattern—a square enclosing a rosette

◀ *Modern Khokhloma tray with traditional decor*

Decorative Khokhloma vase ▶

 occupied in their own cottages, for in this industry as in others, everything has been weighed, measured and counted. The spoon-maker never earns more than just enough to keep body and soul together. It is quite natural," Lenin added, "that ... an industry based on hand skill and traditional division of labour stagnates in its seclusion and immobility."

However, the anonymous painters cherished the traditions of their forefathers. The peasant preserved the true art of Khokhloma in his hovel till the day of the Great October Revolution of 1917.

Folk Artist

VISITORS always crowded around this showcase with its unusual table service which was the most conspicuous of the dozens of porcelain objects. On that particular day, an elderly Frenchman stared long at the set before he finally asked the guide:

"Begging your pardon, but it seems to me Russian craftsmen employed this motif to decorate woodenware."

"Monsieur is not mistaken," was the answer. "This is indeed the one and only attempt ever made to introduce a Khokhloma motif on porcelain."

"Khokhloma, you say! That sounds familiar. Allow me to introduce myself. I am Henri Pierrin of the Arts and Handicrafts Shop. Could Madame kindly tell me the name of the artist? Because, regrettably, Russian craftsmen, out of modesty, never initialled their handiwork."

"This was done by Fyodor Bedin of the Dulevo chinaware factory."

"Could Madame give any particulars about him?"

"A few, sir. The artist is forty-eight and lives in the village of Novo-Pokrovskoye, Gorky Region. He is one of the best Khokhloma craftsmen we have."

The foregoing conversation took place in the Soviet pavilion at the 1937 World Fair. At the time Fyodor Bedin with a team of fellow-craftsmen was busy decorating a new Young Pioneer Palace in the city of Gorky.

He was so worked up that his assistants could hardly recognise him. Usually a quiet and reserved man, he took carping stock of every scroll and flourish

Modern Khokhloma platter

 and when it seemed to him that the ornament was insipid he would make his team do it all over again. The younger artists had not the slightest inkling that this mood derived from sad recollections of the old craftsman's boyhood, invoked by the sight of the roomy, gaily decorated halls, which in a month or two would fill with noisy throngs of happy children.

His childhood games had ended at the age of eleven, when he had been put to work as a farm labourer. But had he had any real childhood at all? From early morning till late at night he coated spoons with clay, lugged firewood and boiled the oil for the varnish. Rarely had he a spare moment to play a game of rounders with his mates. And when he was hired out to work, he had to forgo games entirely because besides fetching water, feeding cattle and caring for the master's child, he again had to prepare spoons for painting.

Painted wooden tableware was made in every home in the village of Bezdeli, or Do-Nothing, as Novo-Pokrovskoye was known before, a name that derived from someone's envious remark that the villagers did nothing, as one could not call daubing plates and spoons with paint work.

Fyodor would have died a farm labourer had it not been for the October Revolution. At the time of the October Revolution's twentieth anniversary Bedin had a proud record of achievement. In the two years of 1936 and 1937 alone he had been awarded a certificate of honour at a regional exhibition, and a diploma and prize at a USSR exhibition, had done work at the Dulevo Factory, had participated in an arts and handicrafts exhibition at the Tretyakov Art Gallery, and, finally, was now decorating the Young Pioneer Palace.

It was his wife's firm conviction, whatever Fyodor might say to the contrary, that they owed their good fortune to a talisman, a photograph.

She may very well have been not so far from the truth. Rather it was not just good fortune but confidence in his own powers, in the rightness of his chosen career that this photograph had brought. "In memory to a brother artist," a great painter had autographed it.

It was in the summer of 1935 that the celebrated Soviet artist, Pyotr Konchalovsky, visited Novo-Pokrovskoye, cradle of Khokhloma art. Earlier he had visited the ancient Russian towns of Novgorod and Pskov. Now he yearned to see the villages in the Volga woods where fugitive serfs and the members of the Old Believers' sect had once lived.

These villages have something all their own, the excellently carved woodwork adorning the cottages. Indeed, every house displays one or another original pattern in the pierced work of its shutters, cornices and window-frames. In Novo-Pokrovskoye, too, splendidly executed carving could be found. How-

Painted wooden bowl. By Fyodor Bedin, veteran Khokhloma craftsman

 ever, there was one house that had no carving. Its smooth walls were decorated with gay flowers and fabulous birds. On stepping across the threshold and seeing the painted floors and ceiling the visitor at once realised that this was the home of a real artist.

Konchalovsky chose to lodge in this house. His host, Fyodor Bedin, was only too delighted to accommodate the Muscovite. The heart-to-heart chats over cups of tea disclosed an identical approach to the creative method, establishing a bond of kinship between them in the three months that Konchalovsky spent in the village. Both loved nature.

"I always learn from forest and field," Fyodor confided to the Moscow artist as they sipped piping hot tea. "I take note of every twig and flower, for I might paint it one day."

"I also never tire of telling the young folk that flowers are the artist's teacher," Konchalovsky explained. "You're right, a thousand times right!"

That twice repeated "right" was for Bedin more precious than the most lavish praise because, at long last, he had decided an argument that had been tormenting him for some fifteen years now.

It was fifteen years ago, in 1920, that Fyodor Bedin, a soldier of the revolutionary army of the Soviet Republic, had returned home. The Civil War was over. The Perekop Isthmus had been taken and the last whiteguard army chased out of the Crimea. The door to a new life now stood wide open. The demobbed Red Army man could not conceive it without paint, brushes and that typical aroma of warm varnish.

At the time the Krasilnikov brothers, Fyodor and Stepan, both pastmasters in Khokhloma ware, lived in Novo-Pokrovskoye. Fyodor asked them to teach him and at first everything progressed splendidly. However, soon endless arguments arose, all pertaining to the creative approach that should be adopted.

Their many years of work for jobbers had accustomed the Krasilnikovs to the "tripe" motif. However, for ex-soldier Bedin, who had so nostalgically yearned for his native places, and who was attracted to living flowers and lush meadow grass, this dead interlace was alien. He defied his instructors and painted the traditional flower motifs on the wooden bowls and platters.

Soon he earned recognition and respect among his fellow villagers. He was even invited to teach the youngsters at the newly-created co-operative. True,

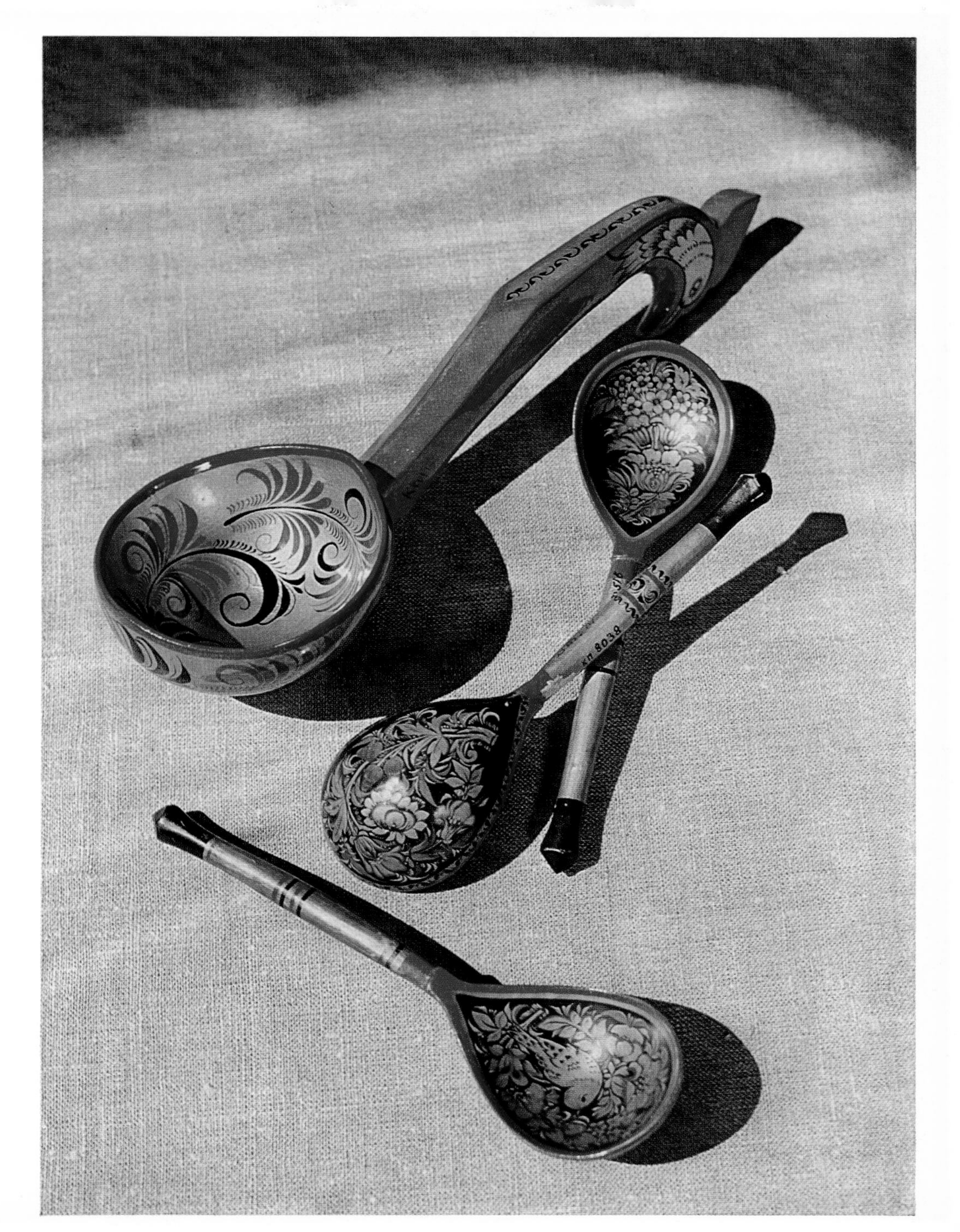

Kokhloma wooden spoons

 now and again repetition of the motifs his forefathers had invented bored him and he would ask himself whether he had done right in defying the Krasilnikovs, since their patterns were at least more novel.

His conversation with Konchalovsky settled these doubts once and for all. One must draw, said the Moscow artist, things everyone can understand and admire. The road Fyodor had chosen was the only right one. There was nothing in the whole world a man cherished more or thought more beautiful than the scenery of his native land.

As he watched Konchalovsky at work, Fyodor came to understand many things. At the time the celebrated artist was painting a new picture called "Folk Artists" showing three young women painting gaily coloured woodenware. The large workroom was flooded with sunshine that one could almost touch. As if vying with the sunlight, the bowls and vases arranged at the foot of the huge white stove gleamed gold, red and green. Looking at the picture Fyodor suddenly realised that the Khokhloma craftsman no longer worked merely for a livelihood. His work had developed into a creative process giving joy to both the maker himself and thousands of others. It would be unpardonable for him now to look at everything around him through the eyes of his forefathers. He would attempt to convey the beauty and richness of Russian scenery in new patterns and designs. At the next exhibition Fyodor entered a vase, platter, playroom chairs and table with a decorative design of ears of grain, clover flowers, bunches of ashberry and spruce branches with honey-hued cones.

Khokhloma had never witnessed such a profusion of colourful patterns.

At that time Bedin received a letter from Konchalovsky in Moscow with a photograph of his picture "Folk Artists". Fyodor pasted both letter and snapshot in the family album as a memento and token of his rebirth as an artist.

So perhaps his wife was right after all.

In 1937 while decorating with typical Khokhloma motifs a set of chinaware for an exposition abroad, he inscribed on a decanter the popular saying: "If you live simply you'll live to a hundred." He took the vessel home and put it up on a shelf where it stood nine whole years before it was taken down. Fyodor was a teetotaller and he broke the "pledge" only because there was good reason for it.

Khokhloma wooden beads

Much had changed in Novo-Pokrovskoye in those nine years. The Krasilnikovs had died and many craftsmen had been killed in the war. Gifted Ivan Smirnov was so cruelly maimed that he could no longer wield a brush. Only Fyodor was left to instruct and counsel the youth. He taught them everything he knew and could do, even divulging his own dreams and plans. Whenever a newcomer observed with surprise that instead of closing up shop, the cooperative had prospered after the war, Bedin would retort:

"Fancy a craft hundreds of years old fading out in our people's state!"

This remark coming from an uneducated peasant craftsman would most likely have astonished the French shopkeeper we mentioned at the beginning of this chapter. But he would have been still more surprised to learn that because of Bedin's selfless devotion to art, adamant belief in the powers and energies of the people and preoccupation with the folk handicrafts, his fellow villagers had elected him to the regional Soviet. Small wonder the old craftsman took down the decanter, filled it with good red wine and invited his friends and neighbours over.

But hardly had they gathered than they began discussing new paints and varnishes. Fyodor's wife finally lost patience and whispered in his ear:

"Why must you talk shop all the time? Isn't there anything else to talk about?"

But nothing could really interest Bedin more. For Fyodor and his guests looked on their beloved craft as the source of all their happiness, their sole interest in life.

Fyodor's eight years as deputy to the regional Soviet broadened his horizons as an artist as well. He addressed himself to new themes and in the new Khokhloma motifs the familiar outline of a bunch of grapes, tea leaf, sunflower and cotton boll are recognised.

The example Fyodor set was soon copied by his numerous pupils. They were, indeed, many, some four hundred, and with their help the ancient craft of Khokhloma ware took on a second lease on life.

Meanwhile the whole environment had a face lift. From dawn till dusk huge lorries piled high with timber raced along the asphalted highway a stone's throw from the village. High tension transmission line towers strode through the clearings in the woods. New houses mushroomed. This transformation of

Handiwork of younger generation at Khokhloma

the decrepit old crone of the Russian village into a young and healthy beauty was indeed a miracle of rejuvenation.

Fyodor's plans pushed into the background all thoughts of retirement. In his preoccupations he somehow missed the day on which his talented pupil Olga Lushina emerged from the chrysalis as a fully fledged master.

For a number of years the gifted girl had learned from Fyodor the methods and secrets he had accumulated over the decades. However, she did not accept everything unreservedly, without criticism. While her teacher preferred an oft-repeated pattern of small detail, she advocated a sweeping stroke that gleamed vividly from afar. Nor did she fancy the cotton boll, grape and sunflower Fyodor had introduced; they seemed too earthly in contrast with the conventionalised bouquets of fabulous plants. She studied the folk ornament and decorative motifs of the Ukraine, Byelorussia and Central Asia and was sure Khokhloma could only profit by borrowing a few points. She even presented several patterns for consideration at the factory.

Since then a talented replenishment of boys and girls fresh out of school has come to the fore. Every new generation tries to profit by the experience and mistakes of the previous generation. Such are the laws of social progress. Today it is the youth who set the tune in new Khokhloma.

Our Contemporaries

TODAY the pedant putting fact before tradition would probably term Khokhloma woodenware Semyonov ware. Because it is the Volga town of Semyonov that is today the main seat of this traditional Russian handicraft.

In the early years of Soviet power a school in artistic woodwork was opened at Semyonov largely due to the efforts of the artist G. P. Matveyev. Its first graduates set up a co-operative of Khokhloma painters there. So this town, once the go-between in the marketing of handicraft products, itself started to turn out lovely objects of folk art. At its museum of local lore which is housed in a fine two-storey brick mansion there is an album of unique photographs including among others a portrait of Matveyev, a snapshot of the tiny wooden cottage, where the co-operative first was set up in 1931, and also a group photograph of its first members.

The Paris World Fair of 1937 won the co-operative wide fame. British, Swedish, French, Italian, Danish and American visitors to the Soviet pavilion purchased tens of thousands of rubles' worth of Semyonov handicraft prod-

300-year-old decor on modern vase ▶

 ucts. Foreign businessmen placed many profitable contracts with the co-operative. No wonder the townsfolk have given it the terse but expressive sobriquet of "Export".

After the war the co-operative was reorganised into a factory with new large workrooms, drying ovens, firing kilns and storehouses. Most of its present personnel—over a thousand strong—are young graduates from the special educational establishment which the factory maintains.

"New times bring new tunes," they say. The modern interior has induced the artists to explore new venues. As a result we have biscuit and cake trays decorated with the ancient, very stylised, but surprisingly ornamental, herb motif. These have been followed by fruit stands, bowls for sweetmeats, and decorative wall platters in gay gleaming crimson, black, and gold. Meanwhile the elegant, painted wooden beads, bangles and brooches have gained wide popularity with Soviet womenfolk.

This 400-year-old gilt woodenware has organically become part and parcel of present-day life, marching in step with today's fashions.

THE BIRCHBARK MYSTERY

he wind whistling through its spreading branches, a graceful birch stands in nostalgic loneliness in the midst of a rolling field of rye. Near the ground its bark is shot with black while the charcoal strokes higher up serve only to emphasise its lovely whiteness. Yonder, by the blue haze of the woods, its younger sisters lean over to admire their reflections in the placid waters of the stream below.

The songs that have been sung to this silver-stemmed Russian beauty! The odes that have been composed in its honour! The pictures of it that talented artists have painted! It is not only admired either. It is also thanked for the good use to which it can be put. At some time in the distant past, a shrewd peasant who knew well its gifts, started on its way a very apt maxim which went roughly like this: "There is a tree that can do four things: give light, muffle groans, cure the sick and keep the body clean." These were, in order, the splinter that lit up the hut, grease for cart axles, bark jars for medicines, and the besom (broom made of twigs).

Incidentally, in 1953, this silver beauty, induced certain historians to revise established views.

Do you know when Europe got its first wallpaper, or rather the distant ancestor of wallpaper that we know today? Till 1950 scholars had claimed that "the custom of the interior decoration of dwellings by means of facing the walls was introduced into Europe by the Moors in the seventeenth century".

However, the birch relics that archaeologists discovered in Novgorod have compelled historians to change their minds. A year after the first bark missives were excavated, archaeologists found bark scrolls that were decorated with either a gay pattern or ornamental openwork. It was estimated that they must be some seven or eight hundred years old.

Intricate, lace-like pattern in birch-bark

A thorough examination warranted the assumption that these were the remains of 11th-12th century "wallpaper". The inhabitants of ancient Novgorod had apparently covered the walls of their dwellings with strips of birchbark having either a painted or openwork ornament.

Art students were thrilled to hear of this discovery, as they hoped it would help them to unravel the mystery of Kurovo-Navolok.

Kurovo-Navolok is the name of a village that stands amidst birch thickets on the bank of the Shemogsa River in Vologda Region. Though there are tens of thousands of villages like it in the USSR, it is unique because only its inhabitants know today how to transform birchbark into objects that seem made of lace.

According to an old custom, in May and June its villagers scour the woods to find a suitable 20-year-old birch tree. Very gingerly they strip an upper layer of the swollen bark. This done, tribute is taken of more birches, the process being repeated day after day until a goodly stock has been laid in to last the year round. The bark is then spread out on tables and denuded of a gossamer thin upper layer and all excrescences. What is left is sandpapered and polished.

The ronwork pattern on this 17th-century wooden casket from Veliky Ustyug resembles birchbark carving

With an experienced hand, the master carver cuts a rectangular piece. Using a bluntish cobbler's awl he impresses on it a pattern of interweaving flowers, spruce twigs or a simple garland of rhomboids and triangles. Then he employs a very sharp knife to slice away all that is superfluous. Inch after inch he produces exquisite lace-like stuff which is glued onto a previously prepared casket, cigarette case or tea caddy, in very much the same way as the townsfolk of old Novgorod "wallpapered" their houses.

It was this curious coincidence that attracted the attention of the art scholar. Perhaps this archaeological find would now provide the answer to the riddle of why only the villagers of Kurovo-Navolok make birchbark objects.

After comparing a present-day map with ancient manuscripts, scholars realised that the Shemogsa River ran along part of the border of the once vast territory which ancient Novgorod ruled. Consequently, Novgorod carving skills could have reached the village, all the more, since it had birchbark in abundance all around.

However, why did this one village, out of the hundreds in Novgorod Region possessing similar ample opportunities for birchbark carving, adopt the craft?

Scholars sought the answer in museums and in the villages of Vologda and Archangel regions in the north of the European USSR.

They found little to encourage them. Table ware and baskets of birchbark, some even decorated with a painted ornament, were found in many villages. However, nothing was discovered in the way of the pierced birchbark tracery they were looking for.

Nor did an overhaul of museum collections provide any clues. True, at the State Museum of History, there is an oval snuffbox of wood, inset on every side with openwork in birchbark. Depicted on its lid in a frame of intricate scroll-work are dogs chasing a stag. The anonymous craftsman inserted tinfoil beneath to throw the picture into bolder relief. Experts dated the object to the first half of the 18th century. There were still some six hundred years in the

"North" platter. Birchbark carving by I. Veprev ▶

 genealogical tree, from the birchbark "wallpaper" of Novgorod to the Shemogsa snuffbox, to be accounted for.

At the same museum are several heavy oak coffers ornamented with ironwork, which merchants took with them on long trips as strongboxes. These dependable, sturdy iron-reinforced coffers, which furthermore had secret locks, were made by artisans of Veliki Ustyug, an ancient town which stood at the hub of major merchant routes for many a decade. The trade route to Siberia and even China passed its churches and temples. So did the road to Archangel, the only sea port Russia had till the beginning of the 18th century. Twice a year its central square was the scene of a fair, to which merchants and tradesmen flocked from all over the country and even the faraway West. According to the chronicles of 1618, even English and Dutch traders had houses in the town.

However, it was not the origin of the Ustyug chests and coffers that interested the art scholars. Their curiosity was aroused by the pattern of the reinforcing ironwork, as it was very similar and, in some cases, analogous to the carved birchbark openwork. A peasant from Kurovo-Navolok may have seen the blacksmith's cunningly contrived decorative work and may have then repeated it in a cheaper and handier material. But it might have been the reverse, as only some ten kilometres separate Veliki Ustyug and Kurovo-Navolok.

When Peter the Great established his capital on the Neva, the pattern of commercial routes changed. Roads leading through Veliki Ustyug to Siberia and Archangel overgrew with grass. There were no more fairs and life regressed into a humdrum provincialism. The making of coffers and chests stopped. However, carving in birchbark continued. As I noted earlier, in the museums are carved wooden snuffboxes and chests inset with birchbark openwork dating back to the mid-eighteenth century. This original craft prospered, attracting more and more artisans. Curiously enough, some half the villagers of Kurovo-Navolok bore the name of Veprev, and all made objects ornamented with birchbark tracery. Anyone asking the name of the father of this craft would always be told that it was Veprev.

However, this was a question that was very rarely put, because apart from the jobber few visited this backwoods village. Indeed few knew it existed at all. Meanwhile the blood-sucking jobber readily acquired for a song the products of the peasant craftsmen and resold them at a prohibitive price abroad.

Glove box, 1949. By N. Skubenko. Detail

In the eyes of a Frenchman or American these lovely objects seemed to hail from a distant fairyland world of snow.

The glove boxes Ivan Veprev made were held in particularly high repute in Paris and New York. At the Paris World Fair of 1900, he took a medal and certificate of honour for the birchbark objects he exhibited there. His favourite design was one in which large flowers interlocked with slender, fancifully winding stems and leaves.

The gifted carver never kept the secrets of his craft behind lock and key, which I suppose is the distinction between the real artist and the potboiler. His home was always wide open to all desirous of learning this wonderful handicraft, whether barefoot urchins or dignified, bearded peasants. However, his favourite, most talented pupils were his own boy, Alexander, and the neighbour's son Nikolai, whose surname was also Veprev.

Ivan Veprev, unfortunately, did not live to see the 1917 October Revolution. However, his pupil Nikolai Veprev was elected chairman of the first co-operative of Shemogsa birchbark carvers, set up in Kurovo-Navolok in 1918. To keep abreast of the changing times, the craftsman introduced the hammer and sickle in a geometric grille or a Kremlin tower in a floral ornament.

These original caskets, needlework boxes and tea caddies soon earned popular appreciation and approval as they were both handsome and inexpensive. The co-operative prospered and its membership grew. By 1934 it already had ninety craftsmen, all bearing the surname of Veprev.

The methods of birchbark carving were handed down from generation to generation. Meanwhile the novelties co-operative chairman Nikolai Veprev tried to introduce encountered resistance from the older craftsmen as being at variance with the traditional precepts.

Blind adherence to obsolete customs often obstructs the advent of the new. First to realise this in Kurovo-Navolok was the co-operative chairman himself. As a result he resigned and moved to the neighbouring village of Panshino to establish another, second co-operative of birchbark carvers. He gave this new artel, whose members were young men and women from the surrounding villages desirous of mastering this ancient craft, the name of Solidarity, as he believed that the road ahead lay only through concerted effort. Returning home in the evenings after a heavy day's work—he was both carver and instructor—he often dreamed of spreading the craft to many more villages in the neighbourhood and of seeing shops selling lovely birchbark objects in veritable abundance. The only jarring note was the hissing epithet of "snake in the grass", with which old workmates from Kurovo-Navolok greeted him more often than not in place of a cheery "hello". The village greybeards could not forgive him the "crime" of divulging the secrets of their forefathers. However his quarrel with his one-time cronies and relatives could not make him abandon his project. The Solidarity Artel began to produce artistic objects in quantity.

Today, some thirty years later, it is hard to say which of the two villages would have gained the upper hand in their undeclared competition. Both produced novel and highly interesting things. Nikolai Veprev created a decorative platter—exhibited, incidentally, at the World Fair of 1937—called "North", which was inset with a picture of gambolling stags. Meanwhile, his "rival", Alexander Veprev, the new chairman of the Shemogsa co-operative, turned out a casket called "The Border Guard", the square top of which depicted a young frontier guard and his dog lying hidden amidst bushes and flowers.

The new generation of carvers that arose after the war, delighted connoisseurs with their handiwork. The delicate birchbark tracery executed by L. M. Balagurovskaya, L. A. Vepreva, the daughter of Alexander Veprev, L. V. Ostroumova, and other artists, won popular admiration at both national and international exhibitions. Then came a day, in the summer of 1958, when a group of visiting Czechoslovak artists took home with them the secrets of birchbark carving.

Possibly in some ten, twenty, thirty or more years from now, historians and art scholars will crack the Kurovo-Navolok mystery and find the missing links.

Birchbark receptacles (tuyeses) from Northern Russia

After all, carved birchbark objects have
been unearthed in Yakutia and
the Northern Urals. At one
or another museum scholars have
brought to light birchbark
openwork which was produced
by serf craftsmen in the eighteenth
century somewhere in the vicinity
of Orel and Kursk. The
day when the mystery will
be a mystery no more,
may really be not so distant.

BONE AND HORN WORK

AGE-OLD MASTERY

Carved Bonework

Near the walls of the Kremlin, on Moscow's Red Square, stands the four-spired building of the State Museum of History. It was there, at an exhibition of Russian decorative art of the 18th and 19th centuries, that what moved me to write this story happened.

I had spent an hour or so roaming from case to case, and admiring the embroideries, the fine work of village potters and glass makers and the skill of Tula and Ural blacksmiths, when I suddenly halted at one showcase, and stood rooted to the spot for quite a while. Displayed in it were exquisite caskets and boxes inlaid with a fine-spun tracery of carved bone. I had known that gossamer-thin thread could be woven into splendid patterns, which could be starched to a rigid stiffness. Here, though, I had before me "lace" affected by neither time nor moisture. I was particularly attracted to an openwork cup, which I seemed to have seen before, but where or when, I could not for the life of me recall. Several days passed before I remembered.

I had been reading of the first Russian embassy to Japan in 1805. It had been an abortive mission, and after cooling his heels for some five months in the emperor's ante-rooms in expectation of an audience, Ambassador Ryazanov had finally packed up and gone home, taking back with him the carved ivory cups ornamented with symbolic presentations of the four seasons that he had intended to present to the Japanese potentate. Could this have been one of the cups that had travelled to Japan, I wondered.

With this idea in mind, I turned up at the museum half an hour before opening time. When the massive doors finally swung open, I impatiently strode through all the rooms up to the second floor.

Again I intently studied the cup. It indeed tallied with the description I had read. However, I had to verify that. I rushed down the stairs and through several long winding corridors to finally find myself in the research staff room, where I inquired how the museum had come to possess the piece which had aroused my curiosity. I was told that it had been acquired from the Tretyakov Art Gallery in May 1955. Accordingly, I made for the gallery on the other side of the Moskva River. Its curator was most obliging and very shortly I had before me the related inventory card which described the ivory cup as follows: "Mounted on a square base, a ribbon-tied bouquet of acanthus leaves supports an egg-shaped vessel. Cut lid has four medallions symbolically depicting the seasons, with four initials for each season. Acquired from the State Hermitage in 1931. Transferred to the State Museum of History in 1955."

The next day I telephoned the Leningrad Hermitage. I learnt that:

"There are reasons to believe that the cup you are interested in travelled with the first Russian embassy to Japan. When the embassy returned, it was kept at the Hermitage till 1931. We still have other similar cups on display at our exhibition of the eighteenth and nineteenth century Russian material culture. They were made by the celebrated Kholmogory carver Nikolai Vereshchagin. This information has been culled from archival documents."

My informant rang off. It would seem as if I now knew all there was to know about this exquisite piece of carved ivory.

Was it really everything, though? Far from it.

Where had this inhabitant of a small village standing on the banks of the Northern Dvina borrowed the motifs for the medallions on the cup's lid? Where had he been trained? And how did he attain such skill? You must realise that his handiwork had been intended as a present for the Emperor of Japan, where the art of ivory carving is centuries old. These were questions that needed to be answered.

I knew, of course, that I could get exhaustive information from experts and monographs. But I wanted to get to the bottom of the matter myself, to taste, if but for a while, the joys of "a discoverer".

I started my quest by trying to find out whether medallions based on themes from ancient history and myths had been made by other carvers. If this were really so, my next objective would be to track down how these themes had reached them.

Again I repaired to the Museum of History which I searched for ivories. In the room dealing with the first half of the eighteenth century I spotted several caskets, snuffboxes, cups, and tankards in carved bone. This did not surprise

me as I knew that bonework was quite fashionable in that period. It was one of Peter the Great's numerous hobbies and quite frequently he carved in bone while discussing matters of state. Moreover, whenever he went to Archangel he always called on the craftsmen of Kholmogory.

In the same room, standing on the floor beneath the arched window, through which one glimpsed a corner tower of the Kremlin, were two chests of drawers inlaid with carved bonework. The fanciful, black-and-green engraved ornamental patterns framed twenty medallions done in relief and depicting cupids, goat-legged satyrs, stags transfixed by feathered arrows and a tangle of serpents.

Most of these themes were repeated in the medallions embellishing the small caskets, snuffboxes and even comb handles. The characteristic rocaille scrollwork was also repeated.

I could see that Vereshchagin was not the only carver to draw upon historical and mythological subjects for ornamental purposes. Kholmogory craftsmen must have borrowed their motifs from one common source.

This, most likely had been a book. So, from the Museum of History I directed my steps straight to the Lenin Library which also has a museum—of books, this time. At ordinary museums though, exhibits are kept

Cup of carved bone. May have travelled to Japan in 1805

 mostly behind lock and key; here even the rarest specimens, unique manuscripts, will be deposited in your hands, should you need it for study. I asked for the catalogue of illustrated books published in the eighteenth century and slowly made my way through the legion of titles, stopping to choose only those which I believed the craftsmen could have used. I narrowed my field of search to some 6-8 books, which did not take long to go through. Finally I came on drawings and themes of the kind I had seen at the Museum of History. Called *Symbols and Emblems*, this book had served folk craftsmen as a source of ornamental motifs.

How had this book reached a remote northern village hundreds of miles away from the then young metropolis on the Neva?

It immediately struck me that the great Russian savant, Mikhail Lomonosov had hailed from these parts. He had once learned his letters from the master carver Ivan Shubny, whose son, the celebrated sculptor Fedot Shubin, later carved a portrait in bone of the illustrious scholar. A Kholmogory craftsman visiting St. Petersburg may have called on Lomonosov and taken away, as a cherished gift, a book carefully wrapped in a piece of white cloth. In years to come the village ancients would gather of an evening in the home of the book's proud possessor and staidly turn the leaves of Lomonosov's invaluable present, smoothing their bushy beards the while.

The story of Kholmogory carving is, indeed, intimately bound up with the name of Russia's first peasant-born Academician. Lomonosov's brother-in-law, the gifted master carver Yevsei Golovin, who incidentally introduced Fedot Shubin to this craft, was the first to attempt to establish a professional school for the training of carvers. In many museums today exquisite objects carved by other of Lomonosov's relatives, another brother-in-law, Fyodor Lopatkin, and the latter's son Ivan can be seen.

Now, after my visit to the library, I had only one last but most important problem to solve. This was: Why is it that the art of bone carving has attained such perfection, mainly, at Kholmogory in the North?

Who or what was to answer that question?

The carvings themselves, perhaps? But they are silent. Only a select few comprehend their tongue. Indeed, only in the hush of the scholar's study, do they shed the veils of mystery. So, I reasoned, I must apply to an archaeologist, as the expert able to decipher the silent language of things.

I found myself in a vaulted room lined with enormous cases. Through the

window I glimpsed the dense traffic and thronged pavements of one of Moscow's
central squares. I myself meanwhile, stood in the presence of Silence, and a reverent awe reduced my voice to a mere whisper, so afraid was I that the witnesses of millennium-old events, now dormant in the shelves, might spring to life.

By the time the archaeologist had completed his story, the neon advertisements outside were flashing blue, green and red, for the hours had sped surreptitiously by while I had been travelling in a mental time machine back into history's dusty past.

Casket of tinted carved bone. Mid-18th century Kholmogory work

As if by wave of a magic wand there appeared before me knives, awls and needles of carved bone, the simple tools of a tailor who had plied his trade thousands of years ago in what is now Kursk Region. Another object, found in Karelia, was a bone dagger with a handle made in the shape of an elk's head.

More and more bone work came off the shelves, the ornamentation increasing in intricacy and the finish becoming more sophisticated. Finally, I was shown a bone box from old Novgorod, the remote progenitor of the wooden pencil-boxes that schoolchildren use today. Its neighbour was a bone comb, the great-grandaunt of the plastic counterpart to be found in any haberdashery shop now.

Though the objects were silent I seemed to hear them tell me the fascinating story of strings of sleighs bringing walrus and mammoth tusks from the snowy North; I seemed to hear the sounds of saws and the creaking of crude lathes, worked by the craftsmen of Kiev and Novgorod from early morning till late at night; and I even seemed to smell the stench of charred bone of which each cottage reeked.

From time to time the jobber came to collect the finished article, which he sold elsewhere at a profit of 1,000 per cent to opulent merchants from abroad, who were eager to acquire these carvings—as Russian bonework ranked in the West on a par with the brightly coloured silks of the Orient and precious gems. No wonder, the twelfth-century Byzantine author Johann Tzetzes composed odes to the carved bone of the Slavs, or Russian ivory, as Europeans named it.

In the first half of the thirteenth century Russia was overrun by innumerable hordes of Tatar horsemen from the East. Towns and villages were put to fire, the rivers and streams went red with human blood, and thousands upon thousands of feet stirred the roadside dust as they plodded into bondage. However, in the distant northern villages, beyond the impassable forests and swamps, which even the princes and boyars of Muscovy had failed to cross, the inhabitants kept their freedom and preserved their time-hallowed customs.

In the fifteenth and sixteenth centuries the lands along the Northern Dvina and the White Sea coast presented a haven for fugitives who dared to flee from the harsh bondage of the Russian nobles. They settled these free territories and built sturdy log cabins. Their only visitors, Novgorod trappers and hunters in quest of fur and walrus tusk, passed on to them the skills of the famed craftsmen of their city. The local folk willingly turned this experience to advantage. To while away the long and weary winter evenings, they carved

18th-century toilet chest of carved bone

 handles for hunting knives, caskets, and fancifully decorated combs, working by the light of primitive oil wicks or wooden torches. Handing the craft down from generation to generation, they both preserved and perfected a folk art that was and is inalienably Russian.

Eventually, Tsar Alexei Mikhailovich, at whose bidding the Armoury was set up, commanded master carvers of Kholmogory to be brought to Moscow. The craftwork of the Shishenin brothers, the Zubkov brothers and others won the admiration of travellers from Europe and was often presented by embassies of the Russian Tsar as gifts to neighbouring potentates.

Ornamental pincushion. First half o 18th century. Kholmogory

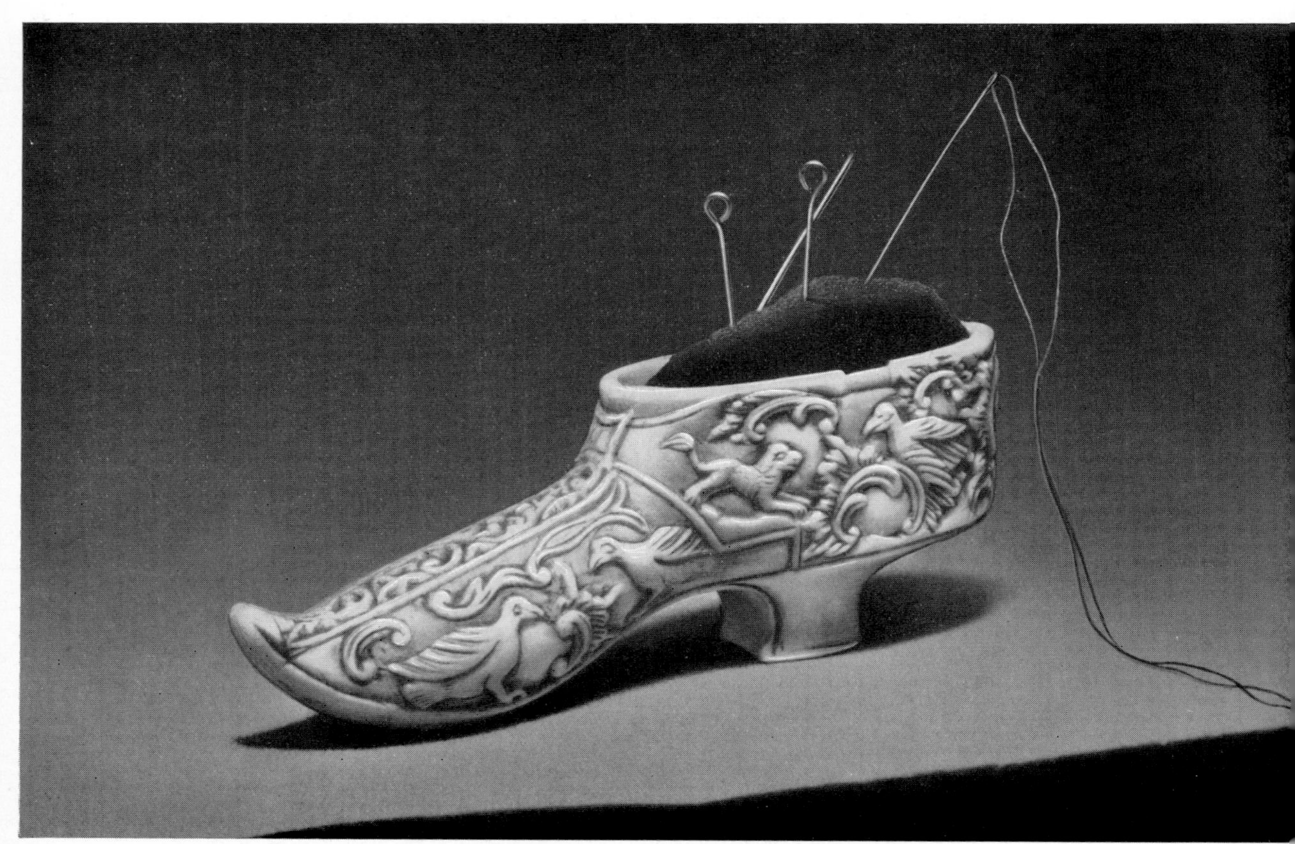

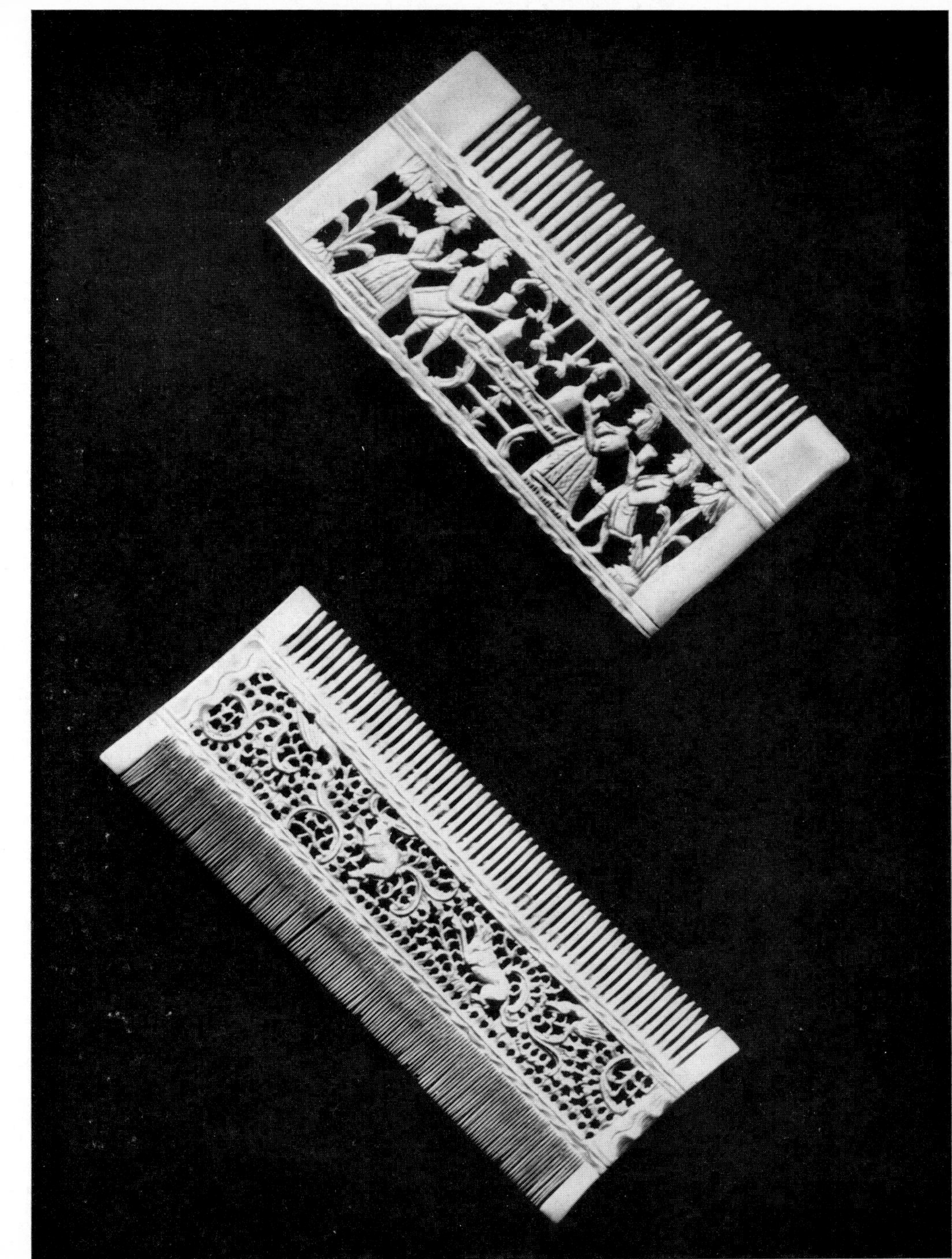

Carved bone combs that were in vogue in the 18th century

Another hundred years went by. The Russian aristocracy sought to outdo the West in extravagance. The craze for ornate adornment and costly bric-a-brac produced a demand for the unique products of the master carvers of Kholmogory. In museums today the material culture of the eighteenth century is extensively represented by exquisite handiwork of the carvers of Archangel Province.

Now at last I knew why the Kholmogory carvers had achieved such consummate perfection.

But that was not all. What vicissitudes had this craft experienced later? I again applied to the library for the answer.

Thumbing through the yellowed pages of old newspapers and magazines, I found recurrent mention of this folk handicraft. In 1868 the Archangel *Provincial News* published a sad brief note commenting on the glorious past of the bone carving industry. "Earlier," said the newspaper, "delicate open-work had been carved out of bone to embellish chests, caskets and commodes. Nests of spheres, icons and even portraits and also combs were made of bone." "But now," the paper summed up, "the craft was almost extinct."

Twenty years later another magazine observed: "The industry has dwindled to negligible proportions. Small caskets, crosses, icons and knives are made. Though an insignificant quantity is produced, one will often see articles of exquisite elegance." The explanation afforded was that, "the peasants take a disadvantageous view of bone carving, considering it difficult to market".

By the close of the nineteenth century the fad for carved bonework had died out. In vain did the craftsmen of Kholmogory produce still more ornately carved ware for fairs. There was no demand.

I was about to go, when I came across General Bibikov's report for 1912—Archangel Province, Its Riches and Needs. This voluminous account dealt with every possible aspect—farming, fishing and even the manufacturing industries. At the tail end, I spotted these few chance lines: "The village of Lomonosovo once possessed a developed carving handicraft, which has waned, though, due to the absence of a demand."

By the time of the 1917 October Revolution, the "Russian ivory" craft, which had aroused such enthusiastic admiration throughout Europe seven centuries earlier, was in complete oblivion.

In my preoccupation with the history of the master carvers of Kholmogory, I have quite forgotten to mention the lot of their brother craftsmen in the

200-year-old snuff-box of carved bone

remote Siberian town of Tobolsk, who won a gold medal at the Paris World Fair in 1900 for their handiwork.

Tobolsk, which was founded in 1587, was one of the tsarist empire's biggest economic, administrative and cultural centres east of the Urals. Siberia's first newspaper and first theatre started there. Many people, exiled for political reasons, including among others Radishchev and the Decembrists W. Kuchelbecker and A. Muravyov (the Decembrists were a group of progressively-minded Russian officers who staged an abortive revolt against the Tsar in St. Petersburg in December 1825), lived there. This was also the birthplace of the great chemist Mendeleyev, the celebrated artist Perov, and the talented

"Krylov Fables" casket of carved bone. Modern craftsmanship by A. Guryev, Kholmogory

composer Alabyev. Mammoth tusks from all over Siberia, a marvellous material for carving, were offered in abundance at the crowded fairs in the city.

Generation after generation of the Khanty and Mansi tribes of Northern Siberia had carved miniature sculptures of animals. It was traditional, before going out on a hunting trip, for the tribesman to utter long incantations before the carved image of a deer, bear or walrus. "Oh great bear," he would chant. "Oh king of bears, be not angry with me should I slay your brother." He would then dip the miniature into tallow and blood, imploring the gods to grant him good luck. Russians who came to populate these parts learned their dimensional carving from the local tribesman, which explains its popularity with the master carvers of Tobolsk.

The carved miniatures of hunters in national costumes, majestic, antlered deer, lumbering bears and crafty foxes invariably commanded a ready sale at fairs in Yekaterinburg (now Sverdlovsk), in Kazan and Kursk, and in Nizhni-Novgorod (now Gorky).

The pink, green and blue price lists of the bone carving workshops established in Tobolsk at the close of the past century, announced that "objects are based on original drawings and motifs borrowed from Siberian life and its flora and fauna". In faded copies of the *Odessa News*, printed in the now forgotten old Russian orthography, I found Maxim Gorky's account of his visit to the Nizhni-Novgorod Fair in 1896. "The handiwork of Russian master carvers," he wrote, "is to be seen in the show windows of Melgunova's workshop in Tobolsk. There are some nice things there, but the price is prohibitive."

Though thousands of roadless miles lay between the craftsmen of Kholmogory and Tobolsk, they shared a common fate. Indeed, folk craftsmen everywhere always depended on the whims and fancies of the powerful.

Desirous of stimulating a dying handicraft, several scholars on the staff of the Tobolsk Provincial Museum begged the Ministry of Agriculture to allocate a small sum "for cash prizes to be awarded to craftsmen for the best handiwork". However, the tsar's officials cold-shouldered the request on the pretext that "an industry of this nature has no serious prospects".

A Letter from Kholmogory

SEVERAL decades have passed since that great day when the peasants and craftsmen of Kholmogory, Tobolsk and thousands of other Russian towns and villages became fully fledged masters of their own country. Today it causes no surprise to see at the many art shows new handicraft products alongside the creations of well-known painters and sculptors, or to find lacemakers from Vologda, potters from Gzhel and master carvers from Kholmogory hobnobbing with members of the USSR Academy of Arts in exposition catalogues.

In one of these catalogues, I came across the name of a man of whom I had heard much. He was Ivan Vereshchagin, a master carver at the Lomonosov factory in the Kholmogory district, Archangel Region, who was born in 1917. This came as a most delightful surprise. It seemed that he was a descendant of the man who had carved the cup which had gone to Japan, that he was also a carver in bone, and also lived in Kholmogory. Since he was born in 1917 his life typified the lot of the Kholmogory master carvers in the new Soviet state.

Indeed, I thought, who could best tell me about the renascence of this craft, if not a man who had himself been instrumental in its rise? I wrote him a letter and soon received a reply on several, neatly folded sheets filled with fine but legible handwriting.

"I got your letter," he wrote, "and am only too happy to answer. You write that you want to know about my forefathers. But what can I really tell you about them? I know very little. True, my grandmother and aunt knew much and had many old objects. But they weren't able to keep all the heirlooms, because, as you know, life was no bed of roses.

"In our family almost everyone could carve in bone, but not all were village folk. My grandfather, for instance, was not so keen on the craft and got himself a job on a shipping line. Father spent most of the day out in the field or in the kitchen garden. And, for good reason, for we had a pretty big family. What's more, bone carving wasn't fancied at the time. So what could father do? Out of all our family only four of us, boys, including myself, liked to carve in bone. True, later, one of the sisters also took up the craft.

"At the time there were only three craftsmen left in Kholmogory who still did carving. These were Vasily Guryev, Vasily Uzikov and Grigory Petrovsky.

"Deer Team." Tobolsk bonework, Siberia

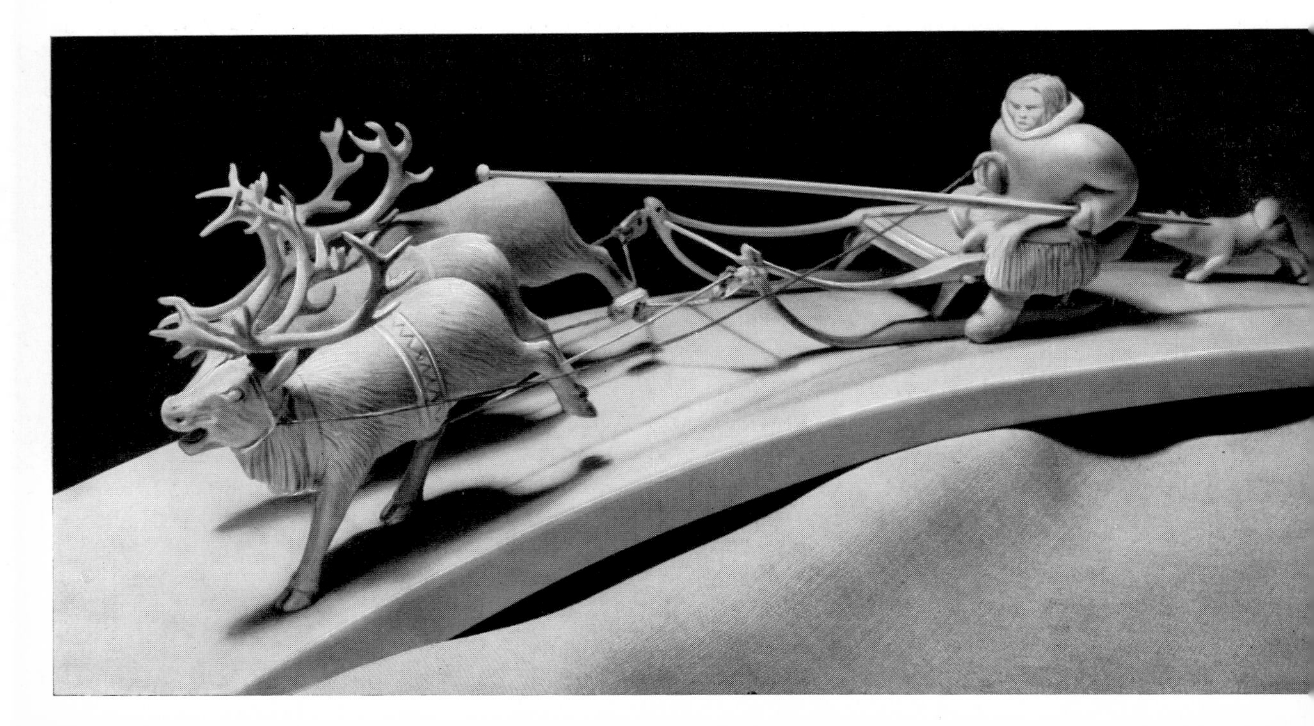

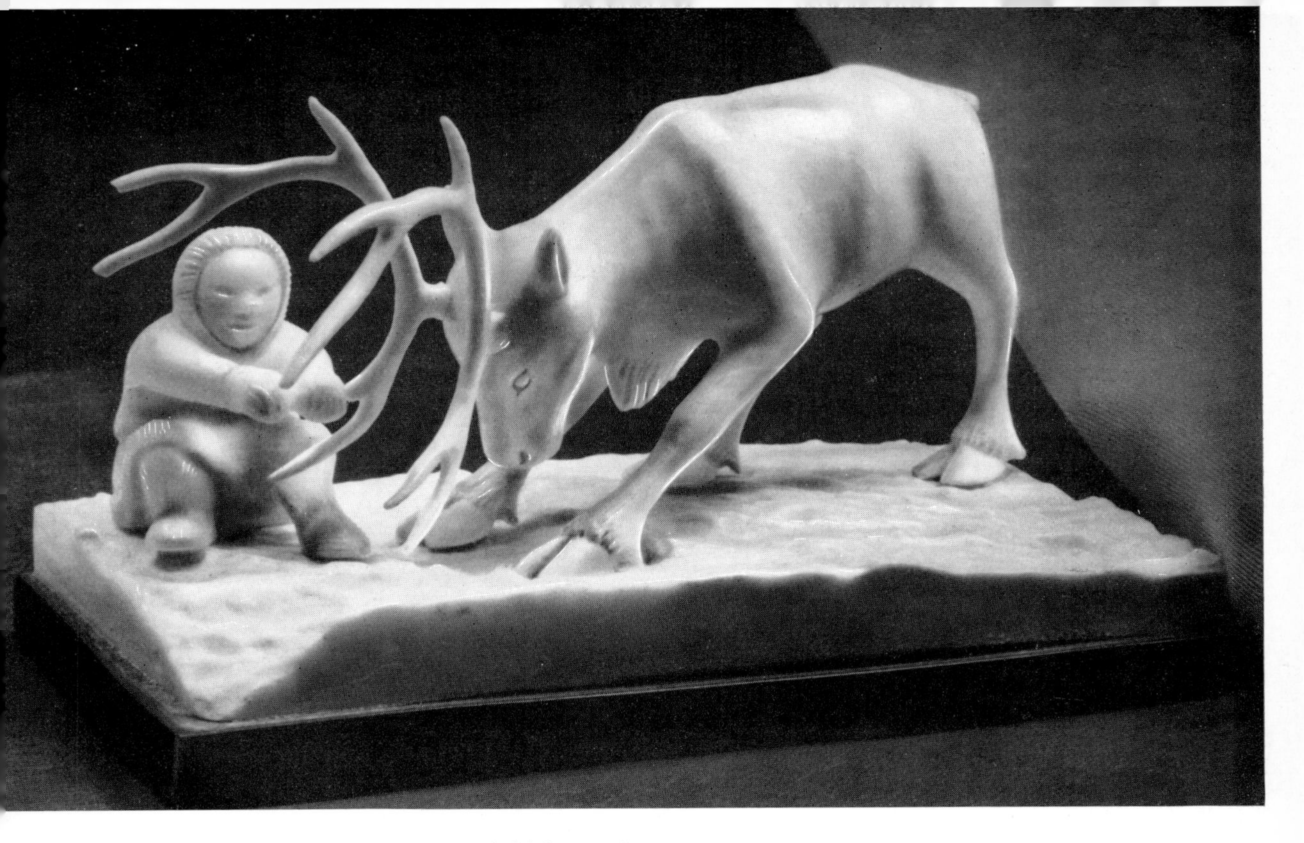

"Young Deer-breeder." By K. Peskov. Tobolsk bonework

When a school in bone carving was started in Lomonosov in the autumn of 1929, the three old men became instructors and I joined their class.

"It so happened that at that time my parents wanted to move into town and take me with them. But as I didn't want to leave the school and give up the craft I liked so much, I stayed behind. I was twelve then.

"My friends helped me. Among the others who learned the craft with me were Timofei Gorbatov, Fyodor Rychkov and Mikhail Khristoforov. Many were killed in the war. However, those who came through will never forget how happy the old craftsmen were when they saw our progress.

"Classes began at nine in the morning and went on till two. We had an hour's break for dinner and then went back to our classes till seven in the evening. In 1932, after three years of schooling, I started out on my own. At first we copied the old specimens and patterns. However, with every year we accumulated experience and more and more craftsmen were trained. Such splendid carvers as Anatoly Shtang and Parfen Chernikovich branched out on their own. Every year ten to fifteen school-leavers joined the co-operative. At that time it was mostly the creations of that wonderful artist Mikhail Rakov which served as prototypes.

"When the war started, I was drafted, because of poor eyesight, into a construction unit that rebuilt nazi destroyed towns. However, a year before the war ended several carvers, myself among them, were demobilised so as to work at the co-op. The government was concerned about keeping the craft alive.

"As for the bonework itself, we elaborated upon the old traditions. However, one can't carve only intricate openwork all the time. One has to invent. And that's what we're doing. We want the new things we are making not only to go to shows and museums, but also to adorn the ordinary Soviet home. Indeed, I must say that the caskets, boxes and picture frames we are now producing could very well decorate any dwelling. In our work we try to reflect life as it is today, and first of all in the North, because we are more familiar with that.

"You also write that you want to know of any new and interesting developments in the work of our craftsmen generally. That's a rather tough question to answer. After all, we've got about a hundred carvers today, not just three as we had at the beginning. So I'll mention only the very best. Chernikovich is finishing a casket and plans to begin a new cup. Shtang is working on a big vase, and Guryev is also starting a cup. Many of the young carvers hope to take themes from Russian fairy-tales.

"Though I'm not feeling too well, I haven't given up work and am busy on a new casket. I've simply listed what we are doing at present. As for the future, we shall continue our searches and try to create new, interesting and beautiful things. Of course we won't forget the old traditions.

"There, I think, I've answered all your questions. If there is anything else you want to know, do write. I shall be only too happy to tell you about life as it is today and as it was in the past. You can find out a lot about the older generation from the master carver Lopatkin, who is now nearing ninety. He often likes to reminisce about the way they used to work before.

"If you happen to know anything about my forefathers, please write and tell me. Could you give me any photographs of their work? I shall be very grateful.

"Do write, I'll be very glad to hear from you.

"Yours sincerely,
"*Ivan Vereshchägin*"

My correspondent had merely listed the names of the more gifted carvers and their best pieces. This, naturally, did not provide a comprehensive idea of the work of the Kholmogory craftsmen. I had to see the objects themselves. So off I went to the Museum of Arts and Handicrafts in Stanislavsky Street. What caught my attention the moment I stepped into the big exhibition hall was a pierced-work cup of mammoth tusk that was almost the exact replica of Vereshchagin's at the Museum of History. True now, the ornament was still more fanciful and intricate and, instead of symbolical presentations of the seasons, its creator, the craftsman M. Sinkova, had depicted bear- and foxhunting scenes. In the showcase right above this cup were three more which, as I learned from the labels, had been carved by Shtang and Chernikovich.

Carved picture frame of walrus tusk, 1947. By U. Sharypina-Tryapitsina. Kholmogory

The cup, incidentally, was not Chernikovich's only piece on display. Indeed, he had a whole showcase to himself. In the small objects intended as decorations for the home, the famous craftsman had sought to display all the beauty of polished bone. The edges of the smooth sides of his "Dog and Hare" casket are decorated with a coloured engraving which imparts a particular warmth to the bone. Depicted on the lid, in the middle of an ornament of young spruce branches new to Kholmogory motifs, is a dog chasing a hare. The same device was used on his boxes for toilet accessories, a small frame engraved with an ornamental pattern called "The North", and many other pieces.

More in keeping with tradition was the excellent bonework done by Ivan Vereshchagin, Ustinia Sharypina-Tryapitsina and Anatoly Bugayev, to mention but three. The fanciful flourish is still, in their particular case, the basic element of the carved pattern. True, with the passage of years it has become still more intricate, but, at the same time, there is, so to speak, more sense and purpose to it, as now and again it manifests itself as the stem of a fabulous flower or herb. This is especially true of the handiwork of the carver Guryev, whose exquisite miniature openwork boxes seem wreathed of tiny, white flowers with a barely discernible yellowish tinge.

The fact that pieces of boneware executed in diverse styles can stand side by side, effectively demonstrates that the craftsmen of the Lomonosov factory, an enterprise enjoying high repute in the USSR, both cherish the heritage of the past and search for new aesthetic values.

A NEW HANDICRAFT IS BORN

hotkovo is a small town some sixty kilometres north of Moscow near Zagorsk, whose inhabitants, as well as the people of the villages in the vicinity, have engaged in wood carving from time immemorial, father passing to son his unsophisticated methods of working a block of lime or aspen. More gifted craftsmen carved small icons from unyielding boxwood and this handicraft—that of working in hard woods—is still extant in the region.

In 1946, just after the war, when hundreds of towns and thousands of villages still lay in ruins on the war-scorched earth architects and designers were already blueprinting recovery. The people sought to return life to normal, to make further progress.

At the very end of 1946, the Council of Ministers of the Russian Federation resolved to establish a new bone carving centre. This was the fruit of painstaking effort on the part of the Research Institute of the Industrial Arts, which had had to answer a number of surprise questions before the decision was finalised.

Question No. 1 was: Who will do the carving?

Carvers working in boxwood, was the answer.

Question No. 2 concerned the medium, since mammoth and walrus tusks were very costly. It was suggested that ordinary beefbone be used and that this material be supplied by the meat-packing plant.

Question No. 3 was: Where? Khotkovo was proposed, firstly, because it was near Zagorsk where the carvers live, secondly, it had a vocational school for woodcarving, which could subsequently be enlarged to train bone carvers as well, and thirdly, it was near Moscow, where it could get the beefbone and sell its products.

I took the train to Khotkovo, and, asking the first casual passerby for directions, was immediately shown the way.

"You see that house on the hilltop, the one with the little turret? That's it."

The dark red two-storey brick house with the turret was the first present made to the newborn craft. There was nothing surprising about that, though. What was amazing was the "dowry", which consisted of the ordinary range of dental drilling machines. It was thought that these machines which easily drill and trim teeth, could be used to work beef bone as well. Their use should make the carvers' painstaking, tiring effort both much easier and quicker. The unusual dowry was received with enthusiasm. However, the enthusiasm was a bit premature. To work in this new medium and employ new methods of carving, coupled with a mechanisation unknown throughout the folk arts generally, the craftsmen had to learn a great deal. They will still show you at the factory specimens of the very first articles produced—bone buttons shaped as snow-flakes or baby spruces, and ear clips and brooches with a presentation in relief of a young branch, berries or flowers. But the craftsmen, who were famed for their boxwood carvings, longed to produce real works of art.

The master carvers of northern Russia and Siberia had their own fine traditions going back through the ages and their own well-trodden roads leading into the future. Khotkovo, however, had no past to draw upon and, thus, had to blaze its own trails.

The Kholmogory and Tobolsk carvers had had such a wonderful medium to work in, the huge walrus and mammoth tusks; meanwhile Khotkovo crafts-men had only beefbone, which at the best yielded a plate only five or six millimetres thick.

Vladimir Loginov, a past-master in the art of carving, spent hours working his small circular saw through the bone and casting aside the knuckle as so much waste.

Days turned into months and he still had not got beyond the same old round of wafer-thin plates. One day, however, a knuckle jutting out of the waste reminded Loginov for some reason of a mossy old tree stump. This fleeting impression was enough. He was as happy as an actor is, when a chance look at a casual passerby supplies the missing gesture needed to consummate his work on a new role.

To the craftsman, the "tree stump" appeared as a stage for animals to act some definite role. But what kind of role? He racked his brains hard before he finally plumped for Krylov's fables. Now a young bushy spruce towered

above the old tree stump. Perched on one of its branches was the silly crow with the lump of cheese in its beak. Below, at the foot of the stump, sly Reynard the Fox licked its chops. The crafty deceiver was just three centimetres long, the vain crow still tinier.

At the outset, Loginov kept his first ever dimensional piece of ordinary beefbone a secret, showing it to his mates only when he realised he had really achieved something. That was the first step.

Loginov was followed by Fyodor Mozikov, Vasily Kalmykov, and Konstantin Zorilov, the last emulating Loginov with a similar composition based on another of Krylov's fables, notably, "The Fox and the Crane". No chance coincidence that, since both had learned the craft from one and the same top-notch Zagorsk boxwood carver, a man who had given them much and first and foremost, had instilled in them a devotion to their craft.

Engraved beads and tray of carved bone. By I. Karakhan

At work Zorilov is oblivious of all else, concentrated wholly on the mystery he is performing. He will take up a finished piece, fondle it, examine it from every angle, store it away, then take it out again, make one or two more incisions, and only then start a new piece.

Perhaps because he did not welcome intruders, or perhaps because of a habit developed over ten years of soldiering in the Soviet Far East, he was rather gruff, shooting out abrupt answers.

"Yes," he said, "Khrustachyov was my teacher. I dreamed of wood carving when still a kid. Father was a cabinet-maker. Loginov was my chum at school, and my neighbour at work in Zagorsk right up to 1938. Then they drafted me into the army. I served in the Far East, on the Kuriles and Kamchatka. In '49 I came right back here."

And he reverted to his work—as though I wasn't there. However, some ten or fifteen minutes later, he suddenly blurted out:

"I say, do you play chess?"

"Well, a little."

I was surprised.

"Then look at this." He pulled out a drawer, and inside a box, I saw wrapped in cotton wool an amazing set of chess—trumpeting elephants, earth-pawing bisons and faint-hearted bunnies.

"These cowards are pawns. But they're not quite to my liking. I think the others better." With that remark he unwrapped several kid goats, to which he had imparted a butting stance. "That's what the pawns'll be like," he added.

What struck me most, though, was a medium that seemed most unusual for a bone carver. Spattered with white bone dust were several objects of polished nutwood.

Working in hard woods, I learned, scarcely differed from bone carving. Zorilov was first to think of wedding bone to wood. His several experiments were quite successful. He produced a wooden casket, with an openwork bone plate inset on the lid, something neither Kholmogory nor Tobolsk craftsmen had ever made.

The other carvers followed suit. Dmitry Skubenko's oval papier-mâché box, inset with carved bone silhouettes of girl skaters, and the young girl carver Margarita Drozdova's "Grape-Picking" box, received honourable mention at a USSR exhibition.

Several months passed. A wide assortment of caskets and boxes, decorated with carved bone insets, had already been produced. Then Loginov introduced another novelty.

It seemed that despite every effort the openwork plate was flat, totally devoid of a dimensional effect. This was most unfortunate, though, of course, all realised that a thickness of five millimetres gave very little scope.

I wonder when and where Loginov hit upon his solution, which was, after all, rather simple. Could it have been at a theatre show? There the wings create the impression of a street receding into the distance, and, though, the entire stage is only several metres deep, one thinks the houses on the backdrop to be far away. Loginov believed a similar effect could be achieved by using several plates. This suggested the "Michurin" casket, in which the top plate served as the frame for the entire scene, the middle one was used to depict the personages, and the back one was employed to give the background of trees overheavy with ripe fruit. These plates were glued together, the resulting inset producing a scene that had perspective and depth.

The medium, however, continued to cramp the artist's initiative. It was as if one tried to play football on a tennis court. Then—why hide it—the news of more beefbone carving centres in the Far Eastern Maritime Territory, Buryat-Mongolia and the Altai came as something of a blow to the Khotkovo craftsmen. After all, an artist, and not only artist for that matter, likes to feel that he is the only one in the field. Now Khotkovo craftsmen had competitors.

Zorilov worked out the solution. He suggested miniature sculptures in hard woods. He contended that since the amount of available mammoth and walrus tusk was diminishing and that beefbone

Pencil-holder of beefbone. Postwar craftsmanship. By K. Dmitriev. Khotkovo

 would not do for every object, such hard woods, as boxwood for instance, presented a rewarding medium, which would give Khotkovo the lead again.

Soon the factory produced an extensive choice of elegant tea caddies, powder compacts, sugar bowls and small boxes in polished boxwood. Zorilov turned out cleverly carved miniatures of various animals by the dozen.

I learned the whole story from the talented carver Anatoly Maslov. The workday was over and Zorilov, after a spot of chess, had gone home. Anatoly and I lingered, talking of Zorilov's skill and novelties.

"He's crazy about hunting," Maslov said. "Every Sunday he takes down his two-bore fowling piece and makes for the woods. He's certainly got a good eye for nature, and that's why his little animals are so first rate."

Maslov waxed eloquent as he talked of his workmates, their searches and aspirations. But he said not a word about himself, even though I saw on the table, right in front of him, a most unusual wooden casket. The lid was tinted the colour of an evening sky before a thunderstorm; on it white bone peewits darted above similarly white bone reeds. The bone was so well run into the wood that I could not discover the tiniest crack even with a magnifying glass, let alone feel it with my fingers.

"That's nothing much," Maslov shrugged, noticing my amazement, "just the ordinary inlay."

It was indeed inlaid work, an ancient craft which the master workers of Khotkovo, led by Maslov, had revived.

"After four years at the factory," Maslov went on, "they drafted me into the army. My unit happened to be stationed in the Transcarpathians, where nearly everyone goes in for wood carving. It was the hobby, too, of the colonel, our commanding officer. After returning from leave, I took back to the unit a dentist's drilling machine and beefbone. Our colonel, it seems, had learned how to do inlaid work from the local folk. He taught me the craft, while I showed him how to carve in bone. The local folk use wood for their inlays, you see, but I decided to use bone."

"Anatoly," I intervened, "I can see you learned something in the Transcarpathians. But couldn't Kholmogory carvers teach you a thing or two as well?"

"Certainly! Only I think Vladimir Zudenkov knows more about that. He's my rival, you know!"

"Rival? What do you mean by that?"

"Oh, I'm just joking. We used to study together. And both of us joined the factory in 1950. It was about the same time that we were drafted. Then we both came back to this place and we both take part in amateur art activities, reciting poetry. I like Tvardovsky very much, but Vladimir stole a march on me, so I had to learn some other poems. Isn't that a rival? He visited Kholmogory where he learned a few things."

I moved over to Zudenkov's table. Though Vladimir, a slim, spare-limbed, volatile person, spoke fast, his every word was to the point, as if he had known what I was going to ask him beforehand and had prepared all the answers. As a result, I heard a very pithy, short lecture on the present state of bone carving.

"Can one compare Khotkovo with Kolmogory, is that what you want to know? Well, Khotkovo's only in its infancy, in swaddling clothes as yet. Then we work in another medium and have different traditions and methods. Khotkovo craftsmen take wood as the starting point, so I think you can't make comparisons. Indeed, can one compare an Orlov trotter with a dog

Chessmen of boxwood. By Konstantin Zorilov, Khotkovo

team? On the other hand, there certainly is something we could learn from each other, and there's no reason why we shouldn't do so. Kholmogory carvers came here to look at our new machinery and see what we're doing. When they left they said that we, Khotkovo craftsmen, could no longer be looked upon as youngsters in the bone carving field.

"We can learn from Kholmogory, too. Though our craftsmen have blazed new trails, in technique we're a bit behind. Our ornamental motifs, a twig bearing berries, or a flower, say, are coarser in execution, which means we've got to learn. It's never too late to learn—from museums and books, as well as from other craftsmen and nature itself. The artist's mastery grows with every successful incision. After all, we are artists."

Zudenkov resumed his work. Looking at his new group based on the Krylov fable about the conceited cuckoo and smug cockerel, I couldn't but agree. Khotkovo craftsmen are, indeed, real artists.

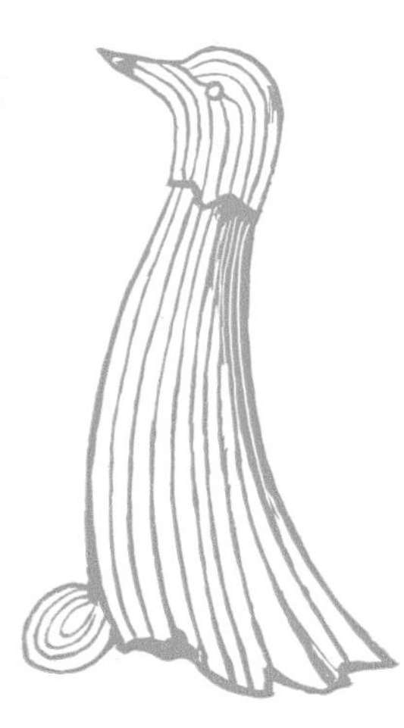

NEW MEDIUM

t shops specialising in the arts and handicrafts and at various exhibitions of applied art, one often comes across stylised miniatures of a bird, walrus, polar bear, sable or marten made of a weird, silvery-brown or pitch-black material. Something in the manner of their execution is reminiscent of the bone carvings of Chukotka, Tobolsk and Yakutia. On the other hand they possess inimitable traits of their own, characteristics that apparently derive from the peculiar features of the medium, which is unlike either bone or stone. One can easily learn the answer by looking at the tag, which reads "Sculptured hornware. Made at the Arts and Handicrafts Shop of the Mikoyan Meat Packing Plant."

Back in the second half of the eighteenth century Russian craftsmen had a particular liking for horn, from which they made various artistic objects. However, the vagaries of quickly changing fashion consigned this medium to oblivion and only some two centuries later did it acquire a second lease on life.

I was so interested in present-day hornware making that I decided to get my information straight from the horse's mouth, so to speak, that is, to go to the meat packing plant itself.

My first impressions were of bright, gleaming walls, of people in white, spotless smocks, and of a host of various signs which said "Sample Room", "Warehouse", "Cloakroom", and "Art Workshop".

Glancing into one of the rooms I saw three young women packing boxes into large crates, whose black letters read: "For Soviet Pavilion at International Fair." I introduced myself and asked whether I could take a look round. I was told that the chief artist had been called to the Ministry of Culture and that if I had no objections one of the carvers would show me around. I was only too delighted and was introduced to Yuri Sluvis, the workshop's top craftsman, as I was told.

In 1952, Sluvis said, Pavel Velichko, manager of one of the meat packing plant's subsidiaries, had conceived an original plan. It is now practically impossible to say where he got the idea from. It may have been suggested by the polished silver-mounted drinking horn which an old friend of Georgia had presented him, or, perhaps, by the act of quashing a lighted cigarette stump in a horn slightly like a fish in shape. Be that as it may, one morning, his secretary, when tidying up his office, collected a whole pile of sheets filled with drawings. No doodles there, but fancifully shaped, diversely coloured horns and exotic fishes. Later came the order to collect and store away all the horn from the meat packing plant and also to transfer two sausage makers, with a penchant for drawing, to the shop that produced consumer commodities.

The manager sought to transform plain ordinary horn, with its many indescribable tints, ranging from a silvery-white to a thick brownish-black, into diverse handsome objects. Indeed, all one had to do, as Velichko thought, was to polish the horn, neatly scrub out the inside, attach fanciful fins, likewise carved from horn plates, and there you had a fine decorative piece as an ash-tray. The idea was translated into practice. At the plant itself plenty of smokers were only too willing to own such an ornamental piece.

Thus a new craft came into being.

The chief artist at the shop is Ludmila Urtayeva, a graduate from the Moscow College of Industrial Arts. She said that at the outset she really did not know which was harder—to become accustomed to the new medium itself, or to train carvers in the process of the work. Indeed, this viscous, yielding medium demanded particular treatment and new artistic solutions. Immediately the chisel followed the grain, the horn laminated. If the almost ready but unpolished article was not properly greased, it would crack and peel. Then the unevenly distributed colouring and the very unusual form required a fastidious choice of theme. To explain what I mean, imagine a face done in horn with half of it black and the other half white. That simply wouldn't do. On the other hand, a badger with a darkish back and light underbelly might prove to be rather appealing.

The number of carvers grew daily. These were former lathe operators, electricians, secondary school leavers or graduates from vocational and trade schools. Though most had from childhood been attracted to drawing, some even to carving, none had any special art training, because none had ever thought of taking art seriously. So to start production sooner and train carvers

Fabulous bird of horn. May be used as an ashtray. By L. Urtayeva

Walruses. Horn and bone, 1954. By Y. Sluvis

quicker, Urtayeva invited a co-graduate of hers, Mikhail Vozzhinsky, to help. Several capable self-taught carvers also assisted, unnoticeably as it were, inculcating upon the trainees a real good aesthetic taste.

Incidentally, I learned most of the story from Ludmila herself.

Having devoted too much of his work time to me, Yuri Sluvis, my first guide, invited me home to continue our chat and to show me some of his best pieces, which he had displayed at a national art show. The evening of that same day found me in a quiet bylane near Arbat, one of Moscow's central thoroughfares. There, Sluvis introduced me to his wife. She was Ludmila Urtayeva.

The cream tinged wallpaper in their room provided a splendid foil for the tropical fish swimming in the big aquariums that stood on small tables and on top of book cases. On the white tablecloth, I noticed a stunning silvery-green fish carved of horn. I must say I had a most entertaining and fascinating time.

One thing that Sluvis showed me was a miniature seal carved of bone. After letting me look at it for a little while, my host placed next to it another, a wee bit smaller. The first at once seemed crude and clumsy. The second, I learned, was a present from a Chukotka master carver. When he got it, Sluvis, who was an old hand with the chisel now, tried to reproduce it. He thought it wouldn't take him much time, but though he spent far more energy on it than he had ever thought he would, his seal still left a lot to be desired.

That was a most edifying object lesson. Even the happiest reproduction is always as far removed from the original as a photograph of a beauty spot is from the actual thing. Yuri gave me the benefit of one more lesson that he had learned the hard way. He took out of a cupboard a whole row of tiny sculptures, including a charming little fawn, a mother monkey with her young one, and a dolphin breasting the waves. As I was admiring them, he added a lone old walrus, a polar bear, several walruses atop an ice floe, and a marmot.

A miracle seemed to have taken place. The dolphin, fawn and mother monkey with her child now looked static. Meanwhile the walruses, polar bear and marmot produced a dynamic impression. I couldn't tear my eyes away from them, believing half the time I would catch them moving.

While the first group of animals, which the talented craftsman had tried to reproduce in minutest detail, reminded me of lovely stereotyped photographs presenting just one definite stance, the second group, in which only the salient features were given, left me with the feeling that a new fold might appear any moment on the body of the walrus or that the face of the dozing polar bear might twist itself into some new grimace. This was real art, art that demanded generalisation and rejected superfluous detail.

His discovery induced Sluvis to continue his search. The upshot of this was that eleven of the fifty objects he produced, were chosen for a USSR exhibition, and 16 for a world one.

To my personal regret, my rather taciturn host did not confide the "secrets" of his craft to me. The little I was able to glean, I learned from Ludmila. Another piece of information came my way, when a folded sheet of paper accidentally dropped out of Sluvis' pocket.

One must realise that, in contrast to the painter, the sculptor must never forget that his piece has three dimensions and will be viewed from different angles. Hence, he must imagine his entire composition as viewed in more than one plane. As Sluvis is so very efficient in that respect, he does his carving straight off, dispensing completely with all preliminary modelling.

The creased bit of paper I pounced upon had several outline drawings and a long list of names of various beasts and birds, including, among others, the yak, cormorant, platypus, panther and swan. This was actually a list of ideas, which had occurred to the artist wherever he was, when on a bus going to work or out for a Sunday stroll. Whenever he had a new idea, he would pull out the paper, sketch a rough outline, and jot down the name. Thenceforth, it would be just a question of time. When the finished result fully satisfied its exacting, finicky author, he would take out the folded paper and draw a thick cross through his initial sketch to indicate that it had now materialised in horn. Unfortunately I did not see everything he had made, while the many photographs I was shown could not, alas, convey the full picture.

However, as I looked through the snapshots, I couldn't help but put six of them aside. Because though they differed in their manner of execution from Sluvis' style, there was something very familiar about them. This was not their personages, characters from children's fairy-tales, but rather a curious blending of the human figure with an intricate floral ornament, that is characteristic of the Kholmogory scroll. I was not mistaken. These were indeed photographs of the objects made by the Kholmogory carver Victor Kuznetsov, who had now moved to Moscow.

This pupil of one of Russia's oldest schools of folk carving in bone had introduced novel methods in horn carving. He had wedded horn to bone, the Kholmogory type of openwork to the Moscow dimensional sculpture. The six objects, whose photographs I saw, were displayed at a world exhibition.

I thought to myself that I must certainly go back to the meat packing plant to see this young man from Kholmogory, heir to that great art of "Russian ivory". Again I saw the two formidable bronze bulls topping the plant gates. Now, however, I viewed their gleaming horns with respect, as I knew what lovely things could be made from this fearsome weapon of attack.

The horn goes to the art workshop straight from the slaughter house. There it is cleaned and graded. After intently studying its form and colouring, the craftsman lops off a piece of the needed size, using an ordinary circular saw. When enough of these slices are accumulated, the carver sits down at his bench. His tools are an ordinary dental drilling machine run by a small electric motor, and, something that looks like a stiff metal brush, but which is actually a small wooden block on which the drill bits are mounted in holes. Right in front of the craftsman's seat is a suction ventilation hood.

This large room in which there are some twenty craftsmen, sounds like an agitated nest of bumble bees. Now and again the buzz will rise to a discordant shrill whine and then descend into a rumbling bass, as twenty drilling bits bore into the horn or trim its surface. The tiny white clouds rising up above each table are made up of the microscopic particles of horn dust and are drawn into the ventilation shaft.

The carving finished, the article is thoroughly polished by a special machine tool. Only then does the severe-looking white-smocked and white-kerchiefed girl, the quality inspector, okay or reject the piece.

I spotted Victor Kuznetsov by the window. He sat with his back to the door. I was dying to talk to him, but thought it would be rather impertinent to interrupt him at his work. To while away the time till the break, I went from table to table observing with admiration the lovely things that so quickly emerged from the deft hands of the craftsmen. I noticed Mikhail Vozzhinsky putting the finishing touches to a group based on a theme from the fairy-tale "The Silver Hoof", my old friend Yuri Sluvis carving from brownish-black horn an eagle perched on a crag, and the very young Victor Krovopuskov, who had joined the staff straight from the school desk, working on a tiny baby elephant.

I think Kuznetsov must have realised I wanted to see him, because he switched off his motor, tidied his smock, and headed for the door, taking out a cigarette. Two or three minutes later we were busily chatting in the lounge.

"Well, what can I really tell you about myself?" Kuznetsov said, as if thinking out loud. "It's the same old story. After finishing the carving school at Kholmogory, I worked for a while there and then decided to come to Moscow, because I wanted to learn something new. That's why I'm here."

"Do you like it here?"

"Penguins". Hornwork

"Well, I can say one thing: I've learnt a lot. For example, we in Kholmogory never carved in depth, but that's all you see here. Then your Kholmogory carver will turn up his nose at horn. I think it an interesting medium; it's cheap and you can make some nice things from it, that will be quite within reach of the ordinary customer's pocket. However, though I've learned a lot, I'm homesick. I like bone better. You can do some very fancy openwork on it."

I asked Kuznetsov whether he knew the Kholmogory carver Vereshchagin.

"Old man Vereshchagin?" he replied. "Of course I know him. He was my teacher. Well, I can't say he's really old, he's only forty, but they call him the old man because of his character. He likes to do everything his own way. We worked side by side for some four years. At that time he taught me a few things. Now when I go back I shall be able to teach him something. But that's not really so important. The main point is that we are both doing the same thing, that we are both creating beauty."

Kuznetsov went back to his table. The swarm of bumble bees continued their unremitting buzz. Though it was high time for me to go, I couldn't tear myself away, afraid that I might miss some new important discovery.

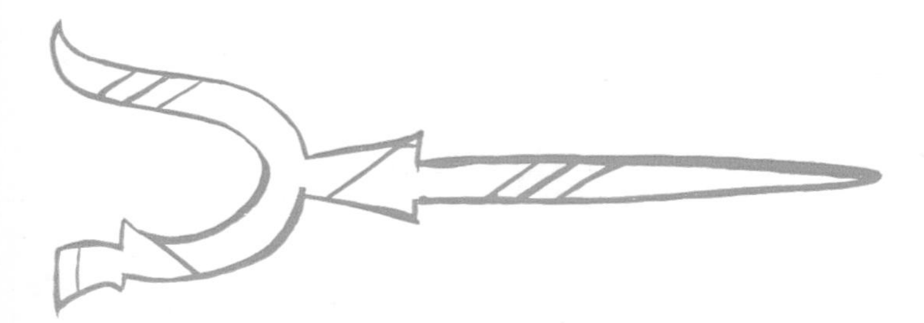

CERAMICS

PAST, PRESENT AND FUTURE

Worth Its Weight in Gold

One can't imagine life today without chinaware. However, some two hundred and fifty years ago, in the early eighteenth century, it was one of Europe's greatest rarities. Fragile cups and vases were imported from the distant Orient. It took merchant caravans years to travel across all of Asia to the shores of the Atlantic. The brave traders had to contend with numerous perils on the way and it was only natural that, safe back home, they sold their goods for their weight in gold. Legend has it that the Grand Elector of Saxony bartered away a full regiment of dragoons for a few china vases.

While merchants braved the hazards and hardships of long journeys, the hundreds of alchemists attached to the numerous European courts vainly strove to discover the "philosopher's stone", that mysterious object reportedly able to transmute any of the baser metals into gold. It so happened that in the course of his search, one of these alchemists, a German by the name of Bettherr, hit upon the secret behind the manufacture of china. That happened in 1709.

Grand Elector August of Saxony, who numbered the alchemist among his courtiers, was happy beyond measure, as costly china could augment his sadly depleted treasury. He did his best to keep the new discovery a secret, moving the alchemist and his assistants to a remote, heavily guarded castle. When Europe's first chinaware manufactory started turning out cups, saucers and vases, marked by two blue crossed swords, the poor inventor was locked in a dungeon.

The years passed, but most European states were still compelled to pay through the nose for porcelain. So in 1744 Empress Elizabeth of Russia commanded Baron Cherkasov to organise the manufacture of chinaware in the country. In a matter of a few weeks, several big sheds and log cabins for the workers mushroomed on the outskirts of St. Petersburg. Everything was ready. All that was lacking was the

Painted majolica kvass jar, 18th century. Gzhel

Painted majolica kvass jars, 18th century. Gzhel

formula. The German, Hunger, and the Russian, Dmitry Vinogradov, were bidden to crack the mystery.

However, Baron Cherkasov soon realised that Hunger "the expert", who had been specially invited to Russia, was nothing but a charlatan and trickster, and he was ignominiously dismissed.

The talented scientist, Dmitry Vinogradov, a friend, incidentally, of that great Russian savant Mikhail Lomonosov, made hundreds of experiments, before he was at last able, in 1747, to write down the chemical formula for the making of porcelain paste.

Centuries later, in 1950, the Soviet scholar, Alexander Saltykov, unearthed some interesting documents exposing Baron Cherkasov. Saltykov learned that a Moscow merchant, one Ivan Grebenshchikov, had discovered the secret of porcelain almost at the same time as Vinogradov.

In early 1747 Grebenshchikov sent the glad tidings to St. Petersburg, together with the first Russian-made porcelain article. However, sensing a dangerous rival, who might pocket the reward the Empress had promised, the crafty baron took advantage of his office and bade Grebenshchikov to cease further experiments and destroy the secret.

Nevertheless, several decades later the country already had a whole host of sundry, big and small, porcelain factories. Most of Russia's potteries were located in the area, whose seat is the small railway station of Gzhel, not far from Moscow.

Gzhel

MENTION of this town is first found in the fourteenth century testament of the Russian Tsar Ivan Kalita, or Money-bags. Thereafter, it featured in successive imperial testaments, as right up to the 1860s Gzhel and the neighbouring villages were under the tsar's direct seigniory. The absence of oppression by the feudal nobility undoubtedly served in some degree to further the craft.

Historians have discovered more interesting archival documents relating to Gzhel. In 1663 the Russian tsar commanded clay to be brought to Moscow from Gzhel for the making of jars and pots for medicinal ointments and salves. Foreign visitors of that period had high praise for the quality of Gzhel clay and the skill of its potters.

Archaeologists have been able to supplement the story historians tell. During excavations, they have unearthed children's clay toys such as cockerels, ducklings and lambs that were made in the fifteenth and sixteenth centuries, and also seventeenth century tableware. Chemical tests proved these objects to have been made from Gzhel clay. This enabled the scholar Alexander Saltykov to retrace the history of Russia's first pottery.

In 1724 the Moscow merchant Afanasy Grebenshchikov opened a pipe and glazed earthenware factory on the outskirts of the city. It has been deduced

200-year-old painted porcelain plate. Anonymous craftsmanship

 from archives that Grebenshchikov hired several experienced Gzhel potters to work for him. He chose a site for his factory near the road to Gzhel, from which Moscow got its kaolin. Preserved in the archives are the many petitions Grebenshchikov lodged with the tsar, in which he desired to have the peasant potters working for him made his chattels. He complained that upon the expiry of their contracted terms of hire, Gzhel potters started their own potteries. By 1770 the villages in Gzhel's vicinity already boasted some 25 potteries producing majolica-ware.

Grebenshchikov's factory shut down in 1774, shortly after an appaling plague, which took great toll of life in Moscow. Meanwhile, the potters of Gzhel both continued and considerably improved upon Grebenshchikov's products. Contemporaries have noted that the kvass jugs, jars and plates produced by these folk craftsmen held pride of place in Russia in this field.

The blue-white tableware was sold all over the country. It was in great demand among the common folk. By the close of the eighteenth century, majolica jars and dishes had fully ousted the previously used pewter and copper articles.

Village craftsmen might have long remained ignorant of how to make porcelain had it not been for something that happened early in the nineteenth century. In 1801 a German, Carl Otto, opened a small porcelain factory at Perovo, near Moscow, on the Gzhel road. He recruited his workers from among the famous potters of Gzhel. Though the factory was soon shut down without producing any real masterpieces, it holds a place of its own in the history of the Russian china industry. To Otto's amazement, after a year of work at his Perovo factory, the Gzhel peasant Pavel Kulikov opened up his own porcelain manufactory in the village of Volodino. Desirous of keeping the stolen secret a secret, the sly craftsman hired only one assistant, an old deaf-mute from a distant village. However, neither the deaf-mute, the massive oak shutters, nor the weighty padlock could protect Kulikov's secret.

One dark, rainy night, when the owner was fast asleep, one Gerasim Khrapunov and Kulikov's neighbour, Ivan Kopeikin, entered the workshop through

The decor of 18th—19th-century kvass jars is similar to that of plates ▶

 the chimney stack. By the flickering light of candles, which they covered with their hands to avoid being noticed by some casual passerby, they hastily sketched the plan of the furnace, pocketed a few samples of the paste and glaze and made their getaway.

The secret was now no longer a secret. In a matter of some twenty years Gzhel and its neighbourhood had become Russia's biggest china-making centre, with dozens of factories, big and small, producing crockery and statuettes, many specimens of which are on display in museums today.

On Display

THE COUNTRY mansion that once belonged to Count Sheremetyev stands on the bank of a pond in Kuskovo, a short distance from Moscow. Its vast halls, ablaze with gilt and cut-glass, house the State Museum of Ceramics; a visit to it is indeed a trip into the past. The very plain, small white bowl on one of the glass shelves, though inconspicuous among the colourful bouquet of gaily decorated plates, cups, vases and figures, attracts the visitor because it is one of Vinogradov's first pieces, the progenitor of renowned Russian porcelain.

Many of the services and china statuettes exhibited in the first few rooms were intended for luxurious apartments. Further on, we see simpler ware, the figurines of dandies, court ladies, exotic Negroes, Chinese and shepherds and shepherdesses in gold-embroidered dress giving way to statuettes of street hawkers and vendors, servants, beggars and peasants—all the work of the many talented, self-taught master potters of Gzhel.

One of the show cases exhibits alongside cobalt-blue cups with crimson roses, the product of the Popov factory, the figure of a monk bearing on his back a young girl in a sheaf of straw. This figure was made in 1821 at the pottery of the Gzhel peasant Nikita Khrapunov, father of Gerasim who stole the porcelain secret. He also produced another figure, or rather teapot, in the shape of a seated monk holding a bottle of vodka.

These figures hobnob with the work of another Gzhel potter, the gifted inventor Afanasy Kiselyov, who was responsible for many novelties introduced in the manufacture of porcelain paste and the painting and firing of chinaware. He, incidentally, was the first to replace the hand-driven potter's wheel by a foot-operated one. His most ingenious invention, though, was his "bronze" ware. We see a row of vases, mugs and jars that seem cast in old, slightly greenish bronze which still gleams in the sun. Only a chipped edge, revealing the white paste, discloses that these articles are actually of kaolin, covered with a special coloured glaze. Later, Kiselyov went into partnership with the Terkhov brothers in opening a porcelain factory in the village of Rechitsa, a manufactory that had won repute throughout Russia. This establishment produced some splendid tableware, as well as statuettes of such celebrated Russian actors of the mid-nineteenth century as Shchepkin, Mochalov and Karatygin.

Several showcases display the produce of smaller potteries. These include a tipsy bearded peasant strumming a balalaika, a pugilist with his fists poised to

Sugar basin. Early Russian china. 1750s. By D. Vinogradov

 strike at his opponent, a tired peasant whetting a scythe, a bearded muzhik carrying a bundle of firewood, and several girls dancing a gay reel. They are typified and stylised in the extreme, painted in only two or three colours, and bear a distant resemblance at times to the ordinary clay toy. There are also some ill-starred imitations of Kiselyov's "bronze" ware. Further on we find a "marble" mug made by the peasant potter Iosif Fedyashin. He mixed clays of different colours to produce the impression of massive but handsome stone. Later, I had the opportunity of actually handling another such mug, an heirloom in the keeping of Fedyashin's daughter Anna, who is now head painter at the Artistic Ceramics Factory in Gzhel.

Let me note, in passing, that an encounter with the past at Gzhel today is quite a run-of-the-mill affair. Everywhere you are bound to overhear the potter's traditional lingo. The local folk have not forgotten the craft of their forefathers.

Ancient Art Still Going Strong

THROUGH a window of my bus I saw a signboard which read: "Novo-Kharitonovo". Giving several blasts on his siren, the driver screeched to a halt, outside a factory, which had huge shops resembling aeroplane hangars.

I got out and as I was wondering which direction to take, I heard a reedy voice exclaim: "Never been here before, I suppose?"

I turned round and saw an old man. His feet, shod in high felt boots, were set wide apart. He leaned on a walking stick polished from long use, as he peered intently at my tie and light leather shoes.

"No, I haven't," I returned.

"Why have you come, I'm curious to know," the old man was only too willing to stop and chat with me.

"You see, I'm interested in chinaware. That's why I'm here," I explained.

"That's all very well, but mind you don't bite off more than you can chew. After all you've got different sorts of china. That factory yonder also turns out china, but it's only insulators for electric wiring. You see how it is. That's why I say that there's china and china. You know what they had here before?

"Girl Water Carrier." China figurine from Gardner potteries. Early 19th century ▶

Genre figurines. Imperial potteries. Early 19th century

 The famous Kuznetsov factory. Heard of it? But today the only factory making crockery's in Kuzayevo. It was Khrapunov's before, the fellow whose grandfather slid down the chimney to pinch the secret. Is that where you'd like to go?"

"Well, I need the factory."

"But sonnie, there's a whole batch of them here, all over the place. They make insulators, plugs, whistles and children's toys, everything. So which one do you want to see?"

"The one where they make the statuettes."

"That's Turygino then. It isn't far away. You cross the vacant lot, where Dunashov used to have his pottery, and on the right you'll see your factory."

They say it's tactless to watch other people quarrelling. But as I entered the office of the factory management I came upon a dainty female, with a motley-coloured kerchief knotted beneath her chin, soundly berating a man who stood head and shoulders above her. I chose to waive the rules of "etiquette" curious to know, why in the face of such a dressing down, the man only swung from foot to foot in confusion, nodding placatingly the while.

Later, when better acquainted with Zinaida Zhadina, the chief technician, I realised she had every right to speak in such imperious tones. She was a veteran at the factory, having come to work there straight from the ceramics school in 1934, when the pottery was first established. Managers and other executives would come and go, but she stayed on, dedicating every ounce of energy to the factory, contributing to each new building and piece of equipment. She can't imagine life without her job. And, by the by, it's no passing fancy, but a real passion for china, that she sucked in with mother's milk.

In the early eighteenth century, in the village of Rechitsa, which is closest to Turygino (Zinaida still lives there), the peasant Zhadin opened a pottery to make earthenware. By 1850 this pottery had developed into a small factory with a staff of fifty workers. It produced chinaware right up to the 1917 Revolution.

Much has changed in Gzhel and its vicinity since. The biggest enterprises and factories were nationalised in 1919, while at the close of the twenties, the last dwarf private enterprises died an inglorious death. However, the knowledge and experience accumulated over the centuries did not perish. The craftsmen united to form the Artistic Ceramics Co-operative and Zhadina, who came

"Bookworm." Caricature of Charles Nodier. 19th centurv

Caricature of Paul de Cocque. Mid-19th century

from a long line of master potters, was taken on fresh from the school bench. She was just the person to explain how porcelain is made.

Before my eyes the small clay prototype gave birth to hundreds of gay glistening sisters. The job started with an operation, the working of which no stranger to the factory would ever be able to fathom. A plaster-of-paris mould was made first. Then the thick porcelain paste was stirred in a huge, revolving, drum-type mixer. Finally, the mass was poured into moulds and transformed into light-grey, as yet dough-like, casts. Each cast was placed in a furnace, the temperature of which was maintained at 800° C, and emerged a hard resonant pink. After its bath of flame, the figure was dipped into another bath of paste, to which a little more quartz had been added, and returned to the furnace the temperature of which was automatically controlled at 1,300° C. This time it came out a gleaming white.

Sometimes, before its second paste bath, the figure is sent off to be painted. I also went to the paint shop. But before I reached it I chanced to hear a fascinating story of the development of china paint.

Paints Story

SUPPOSE you bought a beautifully painted china cup but when you washed it a few times you found to your disgust that the paint had cracked and was peeling off. You swear never to come near anything of the sort again. The preparation of fast colours is certainly very important in the manufacture of chinaware.

Before the 1917 Revolution very few potters knew how to make their own paints. Those that did, naturally kept the process a secret, as one's reputation depended on the quality and diversity of colour. The gold paints bought in Germany were particularly prized. Though some ambitious folk in Gzhel spent all their lives trying to make durable paint, they failed miserably.

After the 1917 Revolution the pottery merchants and factory owners either destroyed their secrets or fled with them. Meanwhile Western firms flatly refused to sell paints to the Soviet Republic. However, one Stepan Tumanov decided to try to develop paints for china and in November 1918, with the help of two assistants, began experimenting. By the close of 1919 he had already obtained the first three paints. The gold paint which he had developed by 1927 was no whit inferior in quality to the imported stuff. He has always thought that man should be able to reproduce all the hues and tints of nature and has worked unceasingly throughout his life to do this.

He is now in charge of a huge laboratory at Dulevo, the USSR's biggest china paint factory already cramped in the multistoreyed building that houses it. Tumanov made tens of thousands of experiments and spent twenty-five years of strenuous effort before he finally achieved his aim—paints that would last for ever.

Today the young chinaware painters at the Gzhel potteries take for granted all the different paints they use and rarely spare a thought for the vast effort it cost dozens of people years ago to develop them. Their only concern is to do the job neatly, because if they make a slip they will spoil the work of many people. So they take great care in claying on the greyish black liquid which acquires the desired colour only after it has gone through the furnace.

Curious, I asked Anna Fedyashina, the chief painter, who particularly designed the various patterns.

"Our two Tatyanas—Dunashova and Yeremina—mostly do that. There they sit, next to each other."

The two Tatyanas indeed work at one table, do one job and as I learned, began at the factory the same year, in 1935. However, their manner of painting differs as widely as their individual characters.

Dunashova is a masterful type of woman, such as in childhood, would always lead her playmates. In 1941 when the war broke out she bade goodbye to the co-operative and her relatives and volunteered for the front. The war over, she returned to rejoin the group of painters. Everything seems to be her business. She may peep into the laboratory, to beg for some new kind of paint, watch a new vase being taken out of the furnace, or simply meander restlessly up and down the studio, sitting down by the side of a young painter now and again to give helpful advice.

Sometimes this Tatyana will retire to the woods or fields to spend many hours in lonely isolation. No one knows what occupies her thoughts then. Later, she will return with an air of quiet concentration, bearing a flower which she will place in a glass of water on the table. In a day or two the flower wilts and one thinks Tatyana has forgotten all about it. Then suddenly she places next to it a vase fresh from the furnace. In the broad, sweeping blue strokes, delineated against the white background, the familiar outline of the now drooping original can be recognised. A week or two passes and Tatyana's new pattern is adopted as a prototype for all the factory's painters to copy.

Tatyana Yeremina is the first Tatyana's absolute opposite. She comes from a long line of potters. Her forefathers owned a small establishment, where they painted white china. She is quiet, shy, and stays at her table all day long, diligently painting intricate patterns using very slender flexuous strokes. The unfired gilt is a barely distinguishable, rusty-brown thread against the blue background. Though it is a bad strain on the eyes to follow the fanciful interlace of scarcely discernible lines, Yeremina feels she cannot give up the colour range she adores.

Despite their differing make-up, the two Tatyanas share one thing in common. Whenever their creative endeavour and skill is mentioned, they both blush in confusion and as one say they are indebted for everything to their teacher Natalya Bessarabova. The other painters of the older generation also pronounce Bessarabova's name with respect. She is often proudly mentioned by Zhadina, by the factory manager Vladimir Toropygin, and by the sculptor Ludmila Azarova, who all associate the flourishing of the potteries with this name.

Meet Natalya Bessarabova

NATALYA BESSARABOVA lives right near the USSR Exhibition of Economic Achievement. At the turn of the century this was where people had their summer residences; today there are tall blocks of flats there and is easily reached by Metro.

The walls of her room are lined with shelves stacked with vases, jars, jugs, mugs, teapots, statuettes and saucers, where eighteenth century porcelain

Modern Gzhel miniature china toys. By L. Azarova

 neighbours with the latest product of the Gzhel potteries. Natalya, an interior decorator by profession, first felt drawn to pottery and ceramics generally, after the war, when she joined the Research Institute of Industrial Arts. On its staff at the time was Alexander Saltykov, who was very keen on ceramics. He had spent many years studying the history of Gzhel and had long dreamed of reviving its erstwhile fame. However, without a gifted artist to execute his designs, he could achieve little. He was delighted when Bessarabova appeared, and agreed to help him.

Day after day they inspected museum collections of Gzhel ceramics. As the scholar traced the history of the article, the artist sketched it, noting the range of colours favoured by the potters of yore. This was actually the reconnoitring of trails for a further overall advance. Thumbing through her sketch books later, Bessarabova clearly saw how generation after generation of village craftsmen had gradually discarded all that was superfluous, and realised how life itself had made them adopt the most suitable forms—with the result that both patterns and colouring changed with the shape. However, now and again she felt baffled. Why, she wondered, had the anonymous craftsman moulded and painted his handiwork in this and no other way? Again she visited museums to study the genre details of life in that epoch. That done, she would sit down at the potter's wheel and, trying to fathom the mental processes of a craftsman who had lived some 150 or 200 years ago, would copy the museum pieces. In this way she often got the answer to her questions. Beaming with satisfaction, she would place the fired and painted replica of the museum exhibit on her shelf at home.

One day, though, she wondered what sort of jug a Gzhel potter would make nowadays. She was well aware that the new conditions, new fashions, and new interiors needed new forms. This, in turn, meant new patterns. Thus there came into being her first original piece—a flower vase. This was soon followed by a jug, teapot and mug.

Though much water has flowed under the bridges since, the factory still produces chinaware based on Bessarabova's prototypes. As I remarked in the beginning, at home the artist has placed excellent replicas of old objects beside present-day blue-white pitchers, milk jugs and vases, and one clearly discerns the bond of kinship between them.

Saltykov's dream has now come true. Whenever Gzhel porcelain is mentioned, Bessarabova always contends that without Saltykov Gzhel would not be what it is today. But the Gzhel potters say, Gzhel would not be flourishing as it is now without Bessarabova.

Who is right? Both. It was Saltykov who infected Bessarabova with his passion for porcelain and who showed her the road to follow, who helped her make the first few steps along this thorny, unblazed trail. Bessarabova was not

Jug with traditional decor. By N. Bessarabova

◄ *"Servant Girl Bathing the Feet of Her Mistress."*
Peasant pottery

"A Droshky." Gzhel china. First half of 19th century

alone in her searchings. She led forwards the factory's young artists, pointing the way. Several months running she spent evening after evening teaching the two Tatyanas, Lydia Chuprunova, Nina Manaikina and many, many others. And when these young people profiting by the experience and knowledge they had gained, made grade, she advised and counselled them.

Gzhel Statuettes

GZHEL was famed not only for its chinaware with its characteristic ornament of cobalt-blue daubs and strokes, but also for its clay dolls.

For long experts had thought that Russia's first china miniature was made at the imperial porcelain factory in the mid-eighteenth century. Only after the last war did Alexander Saltykov provide convincing proof, that back in the seventeenth century, potters in the environs of Moscow had moulded tens of thousands of amusing painted toys with plain ordinary clay—not knowing how to make porcelain.

Glazed earthenware statuettes were turned out in the eighteenth and early nineteenth centuries. Historians claim that in the year of 1814 alone, more than 70,000 were produced. It was these entertaining figurines that fathered the colourful china statuettes now on show at the museum in Kuskovo.

Natalya Bessarabova devoted herself to reviving the traditions of classical Gzhel pottery and had no energy left for the sculptural aspect. Her years told on her and she retired on pension. Alexander Saltykov's untimely death—the result of a hearth attack—prevented him from consummating his mission. It thus fell to the succeeding generation to carry through this task.

One regrets that most folk craftsmen of the past will forever remain nameless. We can only hazard a guess as to what caused them to choose this or that particular shape, form, design or pattern. True, the history of the revival of Gzhel statuettes lifts a corner of the veil that conceals from the layman the inner sanctuary of the creative laboratory. Though, as a rule, the creative artist is most unwilling to describe his searchings, mishaps, meditations and discoveries, it still remains that because of some casual remark, one is sometimes able to peep into this laboratory.

Ludmila Azarova came to work at the Gzhel potteries when Bessarabova had already retired. She was newly out of college and knew little of Gzhel's past and its traditions. Her debut was not auspicious. Her first pieces resembled the very many statuettes that the big state porcelain factories turned out, while at the same time having something of the academic monumentality to which Azarova had become accustomed at college.

One naturally needs time before one is able to view one's own handiwork objectively, and notice every mistake and error. The moment Ludmila could do that, she was assailed by tormenting doubts.

What was she to do next? She realised that she could not emulate the artists working at the big porcelain factories. Competition with such huge establishments was totally out of the question. Nor could she copy objects produced

"Lion." Gzhel china. Late 18th century

"Lady with Peacock." Anonymous pottery. First half of 19th century ▶

"Wife Pulling Off Her Husband's Boots." Gzhel china. Late 18th century

 some 150 or 200 years ago, as popular tastes and notions had changed. Only one thing was clear. This was that the modern Gzhel statuette must be original, and conspicuously individual.

Ludmila spent weeks at museums, intently studying every old porcelain figurine, interested not only in the theme the anonymous village potter had chosen, but also in the methods used to achieve such surprisingly impressive harmony. She observed closely the manner of painting, noting where a few ably applied strokes had breathed life into a doll.

One day she shelved all her previous efforts, perhaps reasoning like this: "Today we find the old Gzhel statuettes of great interest, as they show us the life of the times, what clothes the people wore, what were the customs and habits of the eighteenth century. Sometimes we can even imagine what a definite person was like. Take the old man plaiting a pair of bast shoes, the old woman at her spinning wheel, the docile spouse meekly pulling the boots off her tipsy husband, or finally, the uniformed soldier of the Pavlovsky Imperial Guards Regiment. These are all glimpses of the past that have been handed down to posterity. So what we do today should give future generations a notion of what life and tastes were like in our times."

She soon produced a small sculptural group depicting a young man chatting with his girl friend and supporting his motor bike with one hand.

Instead of painting the figurine all over as was customary, Ludmila applied only two or three strokes of the traditional cobalt-blue to accentuate the gesture and the style of clothing. Thus, came into being the very decorative and supremely national modern Gzhel statuette. More figurines followed: two old women gossiping beside a well, and a girl poultry tender, to mention two. Then came miniatures of animals, objects of which Gzhel potters had been very fond in the past. These included a smug, self-centred pecking rooster, the galloping steed of fairy-tale, an exotic, decorative giraffe, and a wise, yet by no means fearsome, owl.

Can one say the revival of the once famous Gzhel statuette is an established fact? Ludmila herself believes that only the first steps have been taken. This is most likely the case. However, the steps are in the right direction and that is the main thing. We can definitely expect further successes.

Cart wheels rasped and creaked unremittingly from daybreak till sunset. A thick cloud of dust hung above the Istra River and the village of Voskresenskoye, as some 1,500 serfs added to the mound in the river bend, dug a deep moat, erected a double stockade, and put up eight log sentry towers.

It was the summer of 1656.

Some sixty kilometres outside Moscow, a monastery, of a size never seen before in Russia, was being put up at the bidding of Nikon, Patriarch of all Russia. He had commanded the work of construction to proceed with the utmost haste.

At 47, Nikon, once an ordinary Mordvinian peasant, had become in 1652 head of the Russian Orthodox Church and wielded vast influence. Loved and esteemed by Tsar Alexei Mikhailovich, the Patriarch bore the title of "great and sovereign ruler" and "special friend". Nikon was so greatly trusted, that in 1656-67 when the tsar was absent from Moscow he exercised full plentitude of power in all diplomatic and military affairs. An energetic, clever and ambitious person, Nikon sought to put the Russian Patriarch above the Pope of Rome and, by placing the church beyond imperial supervision and tutelage, secure infinite personal authority in the state.

To realise his ambitious schemes, Nikon amassed untold riches. His contemporaries bear evidence that he seized possession of some twenty monasteries and 25,000 peasant households. From the monasteries alone, the Patriarch netted 20,000 rubles annually, a huge sum at the time.

TILES

The Voskresensky, or New Jerusalem, Monastery was to assist Nikon in the attainment of his coveted aims, to exalt the Russian church, and to assert the idea of Moscow being "the third Rome". Nikon wished to erect in Russia an exact replica of the Church in Jerusalem, where according to legend, the body of Jesus is buried.

There was nothing novel in plans to establish a Russian Jerusalem in the state of Muscovy. Tsar Boris Godunov had first conceived it and for that purpose had had a model designed, the required material imported to the Kremlin, and the needed master craftsmen invited. But his death intervened.

As for Nikon, he had apparently entertained dreams of erecting such a monastery the moment he was ordained Patriarch. To further this purpose, he specially despatched to distant Palestine, back in 1654, a trusted agent one Arseny Sukhanov whom he commanded to return with an exact model and description of the shape, dimensions, and ornament of the shrines there. In all likelihood, Nikon also had in his possession the drawings and floorplans of the church in Jerusalem which the Italian, Bernardino Amico, copied in 1596 and subsequently published in Rome in 1609.

Taking measurements of Nikon's temple in 1942-43, the Soviet architect A. V. Shchusev thought of comparing the results with Amico's drawings. They coincided on all points. There is one more curious coincidence: the two monasteries, one in Russia and the other in Palestine, are located on the same meridian.

Though he gave careful thought to the smallest detail and made thorough preparations for the work of construction, Nikon, at the same time, had not the slightest intention of merely imitating the original. In reproducing the design and exterior of the Jerusalem Church of the Holy Sepulchre, he con-

Tiled church frieze. Second half of 17th century

ceived of erecting a still statelier and grander edifice. Thus, instead of the fourteen chapels which the Palestinian temple boasts, Nikon originally thought of introducing 365, one for each day of the year, but ultimately decided upon 29.

The question of exterior and interior decoration also had to be decided. What could be used instead of the costly marble and granite so rare in Russia at the time? Due credit must be given Nikon for his aesthetic taste. He was the first in Russia to command that multicoloured tiles be used as the basis of decoration.

Glazed architectural ceramics had been employed in Russia since the twelfth century. Archaeologists and architects restoring the ancient churches of the principalities of Kiev and Vladimir, unearthed in abundance earthenware tiles with green, yellow and brown glazes. These tiles were used for church floors, and so many of them were made, that according to ancient chronicles, foreign merchants purchased them by the thousand.

The three hundred years of Tatar domination caused a decline in folk handicrafts. A revival in the art of tile making started only at the close of the fifteenth century. Museum collections enable us to trace all the architectural decoration

 favoured by Russian master craftsmen from white carved stone to the five-coloured glazed and fired clay tiles.

At the outset builders in old Russia adopted as a substitute for soft stone carving a set of large bricks with an impressed pattern in relief. However, soon a clever mason, evidently possessing great experience, believed it worth while re-applying the old secrets and covering these decorative bricks with a green glaze. So did the Russian type of tile come into being. It was used to line the cornices of new churches built of white stone, fortress towers, and also stoves in living quarters.

True, these tiles had one serious defect. The reddish clay showed through the thin layer of green glaze, with the result that the entire tile produced the impression of a hodge-podge of rusty stains. Many years passed before tile makers managed to find a solution. This was to coat the clay tile with a thin layer of opaque white then with coloured glazes. Delicate tints of turquoise blue, yellow, green, brown, dark and pale blue, a veritable symphony in colour, were produced by this method.

As the technique of tile making improved, the appearance of the tiles changed. Tile makers were no longer content with a plain, geometric pattern. They decorated their tiles with pictures of plants, flowers, fabulous birds and animals, portraits of the saints, martial episodes and genre scenes.

Patriarch Nikon planned to adorn his temple with tiles and bas-reliefs, of colours that would cause the edifice to blaze like an enormous gem. The foundation pits had just been dug, when a convoy of carts drove in bringing household belongings of 32 first-class tile makers and master carvers that the Patriarch had commandeered from the Iversky Monastery in Valdai for the building of the New Jerusalem Monastery in the village of Voskresenskoye.

In 1654 Nikon, following the practice pursued by many other great Russian noblemen, imported several gifted craftsmen with their families from Byelorussia and domiciled them at the different monasteries of which he was seigneur. Craftsmen living at the Iversky Monastery, included such excellent tile makers as Ignaty Maximov, and Stepan Ivanov who was nicknamed the Half-Devil. Now they were to display their skill in a new place. They were assigned several apprentices who included Osip Ivanov, Fyodor Chika, Pyotr Larionov, Alexei Ivanov and Semyon Trofimov. The talented artist Pyotr Zaborsky was specially invited from the principality of Lithuania to supervise the entire job. As the Patriarch himself noted, this man was a pastmaster in the making of gold,

silver and copper objects, in tile making and in sundry other handiwork. Indeed, when Zaborsky died on July 2, 1665, Nikon commanded that he be interred at the main entrance inside the church, an honour bestowed on very few.

A comparison of the handiwork of Ivan Maximov and Stepan the Half-Devil after they came to work at the New Jerusalem Monastery, and later in Moscow in the eighties and nineties with their earlier work, shows that Pyotr Zaborsky initiated them into many secrets. He not only taught these gifted potters how to make bas-reliefs and high-reliefs in tiles but also gave them a practical demonstration of the use of multicoloured tiles in the decoration of a big building.

The New Jerusalem temple had for the first time in the history of Russia, and most likely of Europe as well, iconostases done not in carved wood but in coloured tiles. There are seven of these huge partitions—some eight odd metres high and about four metres wide—wholly comprised of glazed tiles with designs in relief. Each iconostasis culminates in the tiled head of an angel, while the lacunae for the icons in each tier—of which there may be three or four, depending on the size of the iconostasis—have tiled cherubs above them. In the light of numerous candles, the coloured tiles flashed blue, yellow, green, white and a rusty brown, arousing a sense of awe and exultation among the congregation.

The church portals and arches, with their thick barrel-shaped columns, are faced with large tiles to

Decorative five-tinted tiles with design in relief used for architectural embellishment in late 17th century

Early 17th-century tile from stove in the Ambassadors Hall of the Moscow Kremlin

make a vast composite design of fanciful yellow flowers and herbs in primrose flower bowls depicted against a blue-black background. Each church window is framed with a wide strip of green-yellow-blue tiles climaxed at the top by the tiled head of a lion. The capable craftsmen tried to avoid a repetitive sequence in the frame patterns.

To our regret, it is impossible today to gain a full picture of what the twenty-metre roof which was lined with coloured glaze tiles, was like. In full flight after their rout at the walls of Moscow in December 1941, nazi troops tried to blow up this architectural monument of antiquity, with the result that the roof, campanile, and colonnade around the Holy Sepulchre collapsed in ruins. True, many of the side altars, the underground chapel and the massive walls are intact. Almost intact is the solid, outer frieze consisting of tiles made in the shape of winged angels, of which four hundred of the original five hundred remain. Archival documents tell us that it cost roughly three rubles to make one hundred of these tiles. Considering that several tens of thousands of them were used, one can form a rough estimate of the huge cost of the decorative work. For the sake of comparison, a cow cost only one ruble at the time.

Though this costly ceramic adornment was new for Russia, it did possess traits that were typically Russian. Even today, two hundred years later, one can only marvel at the tenacity with which tradition persists in the folk arts. The tiled lion heads on the walls of the church greatly resemble the white stone lions crouching at the foot of each column of St. Demetrius' Cathedral in Vladimir, which was built by Russian artisans in the twelfth century. They also display a bond of kinship with the wooden folk carving current for many centuries in the Trans-Volga area and Northern Russia.

Still extant in the subterranean church of St. Constantine and St. Helena are two tiled columns, which at a cursory glance seem carved of wood, since they have the same openwork, which saves them from massiveness, the same traditional, symbolic grape-leaves and clusters, and the same ornamental composition of the interlace. At times one unexpectedly spots in the tile design the pictorial presentation of a bright and furious pagan sun.

The craft of architectural ceramics that reached Russia from the West soon acquired its own national distinctions with, moreover, each tile-making centre—and such centres rapidly appeared in the big cities—contributing traits peculiar to each particular city and region. Europe had never known before such a universal application of multicoloured glazed tiles for purposes of architectural embellishment.

Nikon's thirst for power inevitably brought him into conflict with the Tsar and in 1666 he was exiled to St. Ferapont's Monastery in the distant North. His grand project came to a halt. The thirty-two tile makers and master carvers were commandeered by the Tsar for the Armoury.

Thereafter Ivan Maximov and Stepan the Half-Devil made stove tiles for the imperial apartments, as well as gaily patterned tiles for the friezes of the Kremlin chambers and for the private chapel of the new Patriarch. In addition, Stepan the Half-Devil manufactured some several hundred large tiles for the newly completed Church of St. Gregory Neokesariisky in Bolshaya Polyanka in Moscow, in which he repeated the picturesque design of the New Jerusalem Church tiles. Even today, despite the passage of nearly two hundred years, the passerby will invariably pause to admire these wonderful glazed tiles, with their gleaming splashes of blue, green and yellow of the flowers, and luxuriant grass beneath the blazing sun.

The craftsmen of Yaroslavl Region inherited the traditional methods employed in the making and application of coloured tiles. In fact, master potters of Yaroslavl, Pereslavl-Zalessky and Rostov the Great, endeavoured to outdo their opposite numbers living in Goncharnaya Ulitsa (Potters' Street) in Moscow. The craftsmen of the northern towns decorated their churches, monasteries and dwellings with festive ceramic designs. Tile making became so widespread that towards the close of the seventies, even Nikon, the exiled and deposed Patriarch, asked for a tiled stove to be set up in his cell. Whereas the tiles produced by Moscow potters were of a deep blue, green or brown, those made in Veliki Ustyug, Vologda and Yaroslavl seemed to reflect the transparent blue of northern skies, the whiteness of snowy fields and the first unassuming yellow flowers of spring.

Of superb execution, north Russian tiles possess, because of their pastel tints, a lyrical quality, if one may put it that way.

Again, to our deep regret, we still do not know the names of the tile makers. The archives of the towns mentioned still call for thorough study. It may well be that among the numerous documents, a note of hand or the fragment of a record will suddenly be discovered giving the name of a craftsman. After all, scholars did unearth at the Central Archives of Old Documents several years ago a paper bearing upon the delivery of tiles for the Krutitsky Courts, where the Metropolitan of Moscow once had his summer residence. This document gave the names of another two talented Moscow potters, notably Osip Startsev and his son Ivan.

A comparison between the tiles of the Krutitsky chambers and other known specimens have enabled us to establish that the patterned tiles of the Savino-Storozhevsky Monastery, the favourite country residence of Tsar Alexei Mikhailovich, were also made by the Startsevs.

The New Jerusalem Monastery has inscribed one more page in the chronicle of Russian tiles. In 1709 Peter the Great, attracted by Dutch and Hamburg tiles, decided to launch the manufacture of such tiles in Russia. He sent two captured Swedish soldiers, who had been tile makers in civilian life, to the former workshops at New Jerusalem, commanding them urgently to produce enough Dutch tiles for ten stoves. However, as the archives tell us, Peter was displeased with the result. The stoves at Peter's summer palace in St. Petersburg are faced with tiles of Russian workmanship. Despite the Tsar's displeasure, the monas-

The 17th-century tile lion was a popular animal in Russian folk art

terial workshops continued to operate till 1732, supplying, together with Grebenshchikov's potteries in Moscow, countless numbers of painted stove tiles for Moscow's nobility.

Though the Tsar had made specimens of Dutch tiles available, Russian craftsmen soon introduced their own traits, "Russifying" them, as it were. The tiles Peter the Great imported from Europe were white blocks with pictures of the sea, martial episodes, genre scenes, houses and gardens all done in one colour—blue. Russian craftsmen at once endeavoured to introduce the customary five-colour scheme, meanwhile substituting for the frame of straight lines or flourishes the traditional popular floral motive. The scenes chosen were intended not only to serve as a decorative purpose, but also to inform. Subject-matter was borrowed either from illustrated primers and readers, and accidentally observed folk prints, or broadsides, from everyday life, household scenes and even folk songs and old icons.

Tile with fabulous Sirin bird. Late 17th century ▶

Early Russian terracotta tile with apocalyptical beast

Tiled bas-relief, second half of 17th century. By Stepan Polubes (Half-Devil), famous Moscow potter

Late 17th-century tiled stove

Mid-17th-century stove tile

Stove tile. Second half of 18th century

Stove tile. Second half of 18th century

Stove tile. Second half of 18th century

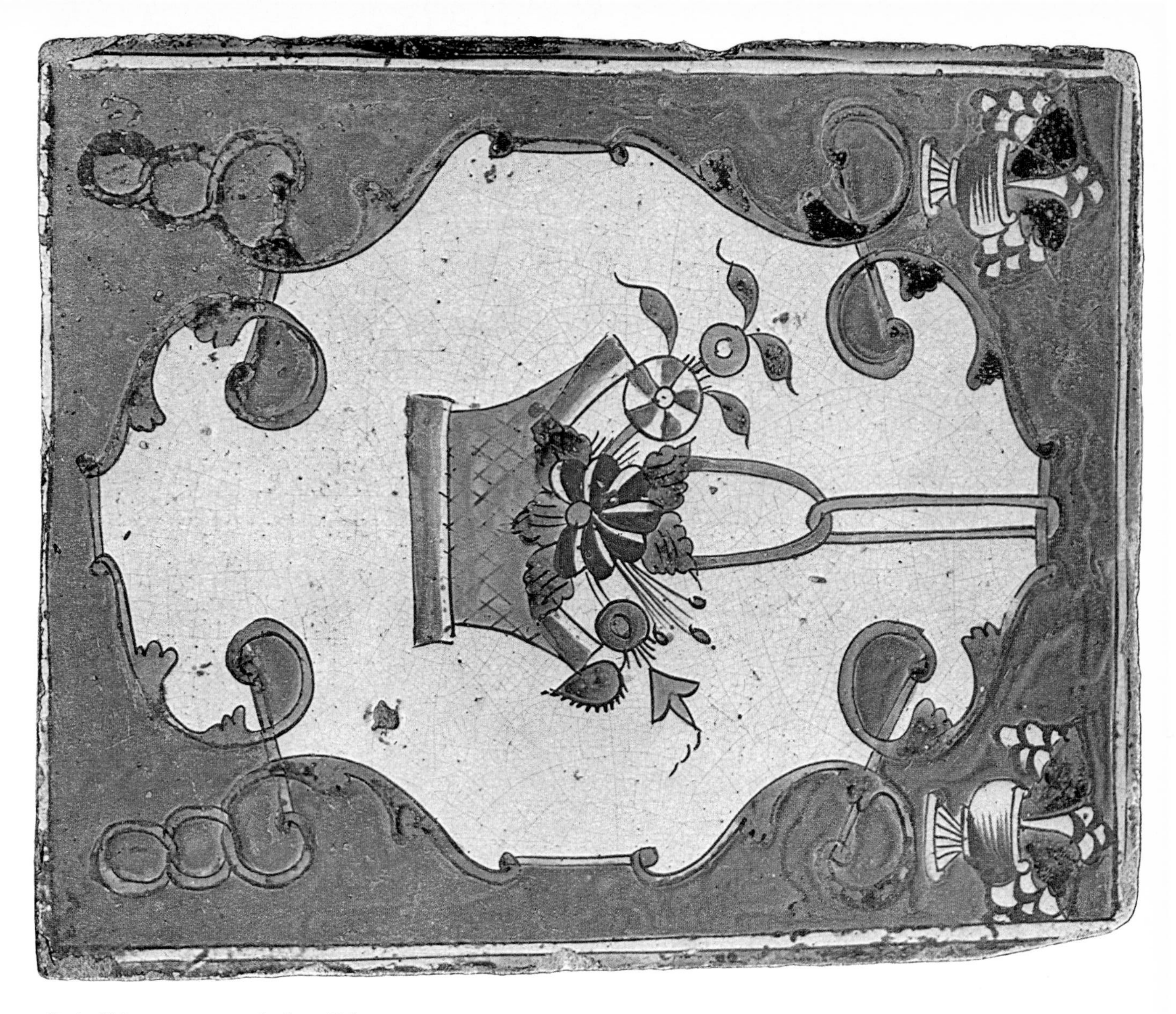

Early 19th-century stove tile from Kaluga

The so-called ethnographic tile was particularly widespread in the eighteenth century. This tile gave a pictorial presentation of people of various nationalities engaged in some customary vocation. But, apparently, not putting much store by the viewer's intelligence, the craftsman would annotate the tile to read: "Persian Merchants", or "Arab Woman", or "French Strolling Player", or even some mysterious "Zhur Tribe". The interest in such pictures was evidently kindled by the growth of Russian commercial dealings abroad, which is probably why the presentation of travellers was also very popular. More often than not these tiles would depict a lone traveller of either sex, with the inscription: "Homeward Bound", or "Going My Way", or "Going to My Place" and the like. Sometimes the picture would be of a person seated on an elephant beneath an umbrella, with the inscription "Carrying the Lazy".

Scenes dealing with music when a man or woman played the violin, flute or balalaika might be entitled "Music Soothes", "My Gay Music", "The Flute Player" or "Playing for Amusement".

Every bit as popular as the "ethnographic" tile was the homiletic one. Thus, the annotation to the picture of a woman hastening with a jug of mead to a rendezvous, would read: "With an offering of mead I go to greet my swain." The inscription appended to the picture of a woman transfixed with one of Cupid's arrows would be: "He has wounded me." The explanation provided in the case of a picture of a seated musing woman, may read: "Too late to repent." Pictures of men usually had gayer and more frivolous annotations. Thus the inscription given beneath the picture of a dancing man might be "Old but gay", while that provided beneath the picture of a man holding a wine cup might read: "Drink and be healthy."

Other favourites were amorous and mythological subjects and also the depiction of various animals and birds.

Stoves lined with such painted tiles served as a kind of primer, even pictorial encyclopaedia. Now and again even the stoves themselves would assume some unusual shape. Several such stoves are still extant. One, to be found in a Suzdal museum, which is housed in what was once the residence of the local bishop, is an intricate six-tiered structure, some three and a half metres high. The lower tier is made of large tiles with recessed arches the truncated corners which are decorated with half-columns. The second tier is of smooth, evenly spaced tiles, laid to afford a very good view of the design of each. The third, fourth, and fifth tiers are completely encircled by the small barrel-shaped columns so characteristic of Russian architecture before Peter the Great. Furthermore, the fourth and fifth tiers have shallow central niches closely resembling the narrow arched windows of old churches. The sixth, top tier is comprised of tiles gradually diminishing in size, the whole affair tapering into a kind of truncated pyramid. The tiers are separated from one another by jutting cornices comprised of small, elongated and semi-oval tiles.

This stove most likely represents the height of eighteenth century tile work, after which the craft, in the final quarter of the century, declined. The Empire style which became all the rage, consigned the multicoloured painted tile to oblivion. True, out in the provinces, where, as a rule, new fashions arrive with considerable delay, tiles were still produced in large quantities for the merchant and lower middle classes. However, this was all that remained of one-time glory.

At the turn of this century, the celebrated Russian artists, Vrubel and Golovin, attempted to revive the old tile making craft. The magnificent fire-places, and enormous ceramic panels that still adorn some of Moscow's buildings attest to their interesting experiments, which were destined to be consummated only today.

Modern tiles have found application in the Metro underground stations, the Moscow swimming pools, the central bus station in Kiev, the Volgograd hydroelectric station and dozens of other public buildings. In the new conditions the old Russian architectural ceramics have re-appeared in a new shape and form.

The editor of a popular pictorial magazine received an interesting letter in the mail. The pale blue envelope contained a coloured photograph and a short note.

The photograph showed a most unusually shaped jug. It was in the form of a bearded centaur, with a club slung over its shoulder and was mounted on a round base. This half-beast half-man bore on its back a multitiered, intricate structure, that served as the neck of the jug. The vessel was of a variegated brown, with patches of light that played on the centaur's sides and chest.

In the appended note, the sender, an Athens University student, said that the vessel was a family heirloom, which his grandfather had acquired in Russia. He wondered why the vessel had the shape of a centaur and wanted to know when such vessels were made in Russia, and where, and why the anonymous craftsman had chosen to mould it as a centaur, an image that belonged to ancient Greek mythology.

The letter aroused keen interest. A member of the staff was asked to gather all the pertinent information. He applied to an authority who invited him home.

"It was made in Skopin, Ryazan Region," the Professor declared, as soon as he saw the photograph. "Look at this," and he opened one of the many cases lining the walls, "and you'll see what Skopin craftsmen could do."

He took down a thick album of photographs showing fancifully shapped figures and vessels.

NEW TIMES AT SKOPIN

"There's the jug. It's Tashcheyev's."

The photograph indeed depicted the twin of the vessel, which the caprices of fate had transported to distant Greece. The old Slavonic tribes had borrowed the image of the centaur from the Greek colonies along the shores of the Black Sea, through the medium of the Scythians.

186 Another source was illuminated Byzantine manuscripts that came to Kiev Rus. In the popular idiom it became a fabulous monster with the bastardised name of Polkan, a mispronunciation of the Russian for "half-horse".

Skopin craftsmen could have taken the phototype from the folk tales or broadside woodcuts of the early nineteenth century.

The next page in the album gave photographs depicting a jar in the shape of a bird of prey, and several extremely curious candlesticks made in the form of a tipsy fiddler and the two-headed imperial eagle.

"These objects were also made by Skopin potters," the Professor explained. "The candlesticks are Zholobov's work. But let me tell you," the scholar continued, "that a photograph gives a very incomplete idea. One must see the real thing. Our Museum of History has a very fine collection of Skopin pottery. Unfortunately, it is not on display now. So take my advice and go to Skopin and see for yourself how they do things. To while away the time on the train, take Yuri Arbat's book *Master Potters* with you! It has a marvellous chapter on Skopin in it. If you find anything that you don't understand, I'll be only too pleased to help you."

Several days later the newsman took the Professor's advice and set out for Skopin.

The first thing one sees on arriving in Skopin are the mounds of waste rock outside the coal pits. A memorial plaque on one of the buildings states that back in 1919 Mikhail Kalinin addressed local miners there, urging them to go all out to help the young Soviet Republic. Displayed on the roll of honour in the central square are pictures of front-ranking workers. One would never think this town was the birthplace of the legendary earthenware centaur. Still, it was the right place to come to for the answer.

The curious newsman had learned something of Skopin's past at the regional museum of local lore in Ryazan. Ever since the twelfth century the inhabitants of the villages located where Skopin now stands, had made good use of the rich beds of light-tinted pottery clays. When the town first started, at the close of the sixteenth century—it was called Ostrozhok then—there was a whole district of

"Dragon" decorative vessel, late 19th-century Skopin pottery, Ryazan Region ▶

"Polkan" (Centaur) vessel, late 19th-century Skopin pottery

"Fiddler" candlestick, early 20th-century Skopin pottery

 potters, who supplied first the closer hamlets and then the villages further away, with bowls, pots, platters, milk jugs and jars, known as the "sinyushki", or "blueys", due to the bluish-black tint which the firing process imparted to them.

As the "blueys" were durable and cheap, they commanded a steady sale and by the early nineteenth century Skopin ware reached out as far away as the markets of Rostov and Taganrog.

A photograph exhibited in one of the rooms of the museum shows a bearded peasant seated on a low bench. He turns a wooden potters' wheel with his left hand and moulds a piece of clay with his right. This is a picture of a Skopin potter at work. Though large porcelain factories had been established in Russia long ago and Gzhel potters were already producing fancifully formed vessels and statuettes, the craftsmen of Skopin still plied the trade as their ancestors did back in the twelfth century. The potter kept his store of clay at home. He mixed and kneaded it with his feet and hands, sat practically on the floor to make his ware, and fired it in a furnace occupying nearly half of his hut. The whole family would contribute. As the men made jars, jugs and bowls the children assisting them, the womenfolk produced objects calling for less exertion, such as toy whistles. Hawking his ware much in the manner of an itinerant peddler, the potter would play a simple tune on a home-made whistle to inform the inhabitants that he had a cartload of pottery for sale. This gave Skopin craftsmen the nickname of "the whistlers".

Craftsmen put their work for public view on their gate posts making a sort of shingle to attract customers. A potter would put out the biggest and loveliest jar he had. His neighbour, observing this advertising gimmick, would work indoors for a couple of days and then place huge spheres on his gate posts. Another neighbour, who fired pipes for the local squire, would outdo the others by producing a pair of lions of the kind he had seen adorning the entrance to the squire's home.

However, there came a day when a still shrewder potter realised that these gimmicks informed only the local folk and that elsewhere people knew nothing of their wares. The next time he set off for the fair, he took his "advertisements" along with him, placing them on top of his cartload of "blueys" as a demonstration of his skill.

However, in Skopin today, there is not one "shingle" left. An old-timer may recollect what wares some of the craftsmen used to place on their gate posts.

The best authority on Skopin's past is Dmitry Zholobov, himself a potter and son of the celebrated maker of the unusual candlesticks mentioned earlier. This old man lives in a new house on the outskirts of the town and is always glad to entertain a guest both with home-brewn *kvass* and the unhurried story of what life used to be like in the neighbourhood and of the objects they used to make.

His father was the first in Skopin to display the figure of a beast, a long-maned ferocious-looking lion, with one paw resting on a ball.

True, Fyodor Ovodov, or the Orphan, as the neighbours nicknamed him, produced a still better lion. Mikhail Zholobov, had merely kneaded the clay with his fingers, when he modelled the mane. Fyodor, by forcing the clay through a fine sieve, obtained threads from which he made the mane. Mikhail, naturally, could not take this lying down. How could he, the neighbourhood's No. 1 potter, be outsmarted? At first he took himself off to the tavern to drown his sorrows in drink, but when an idea struck him, he rushed home.

He spent the better half of the night, before he, at last, turned out a most amusing candlestick depicting a tipsy tavern fiddler, with his topper all askew on his bowed head, seated on a stool and playing a doleful tune. The topper had no top, and served to hold the candle. The job done, Zholobov gave a sigh of satisfaction. He was pleased with the result. However, to outdo Ovodov he believed he ought to do one better still.

At the time of this story many craftsmen were already making various figures. Grishanin, Ovodov's apprentice, had produced a jug in the shape of a two-headed imperial eagle. His mate Cheberyashkin, was better at making *kvass* jars. These jars, the body of which is shaped like a spokeless wheel, require a particular knack to make, since the utensil must be both attractive and convenient to handle, and since the inner part of the wheel serves to hold a cooling chunk of ice wrapped in a piece of cloth. After some thought, Zholobov modelled a jar in the form of a two-headed eagle, holding a violin and a bow in its claws, a piece of effrontery that could have easily landed him in jail.

His rivals weren't to be outdone. For his nephew's wedding, Fyodor Ovodov made an earthenware samovar, which he covered with a glistening glaze. Ivan Tashcheyev, meanwhile, produced the fabulous centaur we mentioned at the beginning.

Zholobov was so upset that he stayed indoors for well nigh two months, making roof tiles. His neighbours chuckled. "Look at him," they said, "a good craftsman but wasting his time on trifles." However, the moment he started tiling his roof, the whole town came round to stare. Each tile was different: one depicted a bear playing a concertina, another, an irate general, the third, a wood-owl, the fourth, a viper, the fifth, a sheep, and the sixth, a rooster. Nothing of the kind had ever been seen in Skopin before. Many potters subsequently came to make jugs, *kvass* jars, centaurs and beasts, but no one was ever able to emulate Zholobov's roof tile feat.

The bizarre handiwork of Skopin potters sold well at fairs. Connoisseurs from Moscow and St. Petersburg came to buy curiously shaped vessels, flower vases, and, particularly, jars modelled in the form of a local bird of prey, the "skopa", from which the town derives its name, as well as a whole host of diverse *kvass* jugs made now in the shape of one wheel with round or square sides, now in the shape of two wheels. The spout would often as not be shaped as a snake impaled by the talons of the "skopa", whose wings shrouded the vessel's broad, patterned neck.

Dmitry Zholobov presented one of these *kvass* jars to a visiting professor. Today he does not have a single old object left to show. On the other hand, he remembers very many interesting things which he either heard from his father when a small boy, or which he himself experienced in the course of his long and eventful life.

When World War I broke out in 1914, the Skopin pottery craft died out. Most of the craftsmen were drafted into the army and, furthermore, there was no demand for Skopin ware. Then came the October Revolution of 1917, followed by the Civil War with its chaos and ruin.

Only in 1934 did a few surviving craftsmen muster sufficient forces to start production of earthenware again. The sons of the once famous craftsmen joined the Skopin ceramics co-operative. These were Ivan Maximov, Mikhail Tashcheyev and Dmitry Zholobov himself. They had not forgotten how to make the bizarre objects their fathers had produced. Indeed, how could one forget what one had been accustomed to doing day after day for years on end. Now and again they would produce for museums or exhibitions the centaurs, dragons, *kvass* jugs or flower vases with the "skopa". Ivan Maximov's handiwork was especially delightful. He not only copied old specimens, the work of his forefathers, but also tried to think of something

Decorative kvass jar, early 20th-century Skopin pottery

new, more in keeping with the times. Thus he modelled a *kvass* jug having a five-pointed star inserted in its wheel-shaped body. Then he re-modelled the old flower vase into a desk lamp. He achieved some fine results, but after all, these were unique objects. Meanwhile the co-operative itself produced cartload after cartload of plain, ordinary earthenware.

After the last war, the Industrial Arts Institute decided to revive the craft. A new building was put up for the factory and new equipment was installed. Mikhail Pelyonkin, an old master potter, was invited to supervise the new workshop. One of the "last of the Mohicans", it was for him to initiate the younger generation into the secrets of the craft.

The salient feature of Skopin pottery making is that the object is neither moulded nor modelled on a master-pattern, but made by hand from a kind of clay cord. In the case of an intricate piece, the body, neck and base are made separately. As soon as the clay dries, the craftsman adds ornamentation in the same way as his forefathers did centuries ago, using a pen-knife, stamp or wooden graining tool. The sets of stamps are usually handed down from father to son. It is this two-hundred-year-old tradition that imparts to Skopin pottery its peculiar charm.

Ever since 1949, as yet unique Skopin pieces have been shown at exhibitions both in the USSR and abroad. The medals and certificates won attest to their initial success. New-time Skopin will probably become just as famous as it was in the past.

THE VYATKA TOY

In the ancient Russian town of Vyatka, now Kirov, which stretches for some fifteen kilometres along the banks of the Vyatka River, past and present co-exist in surprisingly peaceful accord. The new is manifested in the racket and roar of engineering plants and hooting of locomotives at the busy railway junction, and in the tall new buildings with their large window panes; but in the lanes and side-streets is a kingdom of wooden houses and vegetable gardens, a domain of tranquil silence.

However, even there the past is steadily yielding to the present. Soon nothing will be left to remind one of the old Vyatka of the artisans, merchants, bureaucratic officials, and jobbers. However, it is as famous as ever for its lovely, inimitable Dymkovo clay toy. The townsfolk proudly claim that these toys are indeed unique, having a centuries-old history.

To say "unique" is perhaps, a bit far-fetched, as at Moscow museums I have seen "relatives" of the Vyatka toy. At the Folk Arts Museum, for instance, I found several clay toys from the Tula village of Filimonovo and a far-away northern village near the Karelian town of Kargopol. Though they all have much in common, depicting the same female type in her bell-shaped skirt, and the same type of horseman with a similar general ornamental motif of sun-symbolising circles and rings, the Filimonovo and Kargopol toys do not possess that consummate perfection of form so characteristic of their Dymkovo sisters. They are more primitive and conventional, nor are the colour schemes as bright. They seem not hundreds of kilometres, but hundreds of years, apart.

I ran into several still more remote ancestors of the Vyatka toy at the Hermitage, the Fine Arts Museum and the Museum of History. These were small statuettes that had been unearthed in the excavation of the

Traditional Vyatka clay toys

 ancient Greek towns along the northern coast of the Black Sea. They bear an amazing resemblance to the clay toys of Kiev Rus and ancient Novgorod, which, in turn, as, for instance, the clay doll made by an eleventh century Kiev toy maker that is exhibited at the Museum of History, look like the as yet unpainted piece that a Vyatka, Kargopol or Filimonovo craftsman might make in his years of apprenticeship.

However, a second, closer look at the Kargopol and Filimonovo toys convinced me that they were much more closely related to the Kiev and Novgorod toys than to the Vyatka one.

Perusing albums and voluminous monographs at the library, I again encountered pictures of the Kiev doll and the three-headed Novgorod clay horse. Now, though, they are annotated not as toys, but as objects of religious worship.

The doll was the goddess, the Protectress of the Hearth, whereas the fantastic, three-headed horse symbolised the three-in-hand of the Sun-God's chariot. Proving this point, historians listed various objects found in archaeological excavations, cited the numerous and most convincing testimonies of travellers and chroniclers, and also pointed to the images of the goddess and the horse that decorate peasant household utensils and embroideries.

Ties with Greek trade markets on the Black Sea coast influenced the culture of Slavonic tribes, and through them, the craftsmanship of ancient Russian sculptors. Excavations in Kiev and Novgorod have unearthed besides the bigger wooden idols miniature clay ones for household use.

Following the introduction of Christianity in Russia, most of these clay images of pagan gods assumed the innocuous disguise of a toy, which saved them from destruction and their owners from persecution by the Orthodox Church. We still call the creations of Vyatka craftsmen toys, though, I suppose, no parent would let his child play with these motley-coloured clay dolls, horses or birds. Even Vyatka toy makers themselves do not allow that.

Shaking off the hypnotic influence of the word "toy", one will at once trace most distinctly the entire genealogy of Vyatka earthenware sculpture, which goes all the way from the pagan gods of old to the gay, decorative figures of

"At the Well." Vyatka genre scene ▶

 today. Still, one is puzzled. How did this object of worship come to survive in Vyatka? And why? And how did it happen to turn up there, so far away from the historical centres of Russian culture?

The historian and the linguist supply the answer. One can still hear the Novgorod dialect in the North of the Archangel Region and along the shores of the Arctic Ocean. The log cabins built there today are very much like those that Novgoroders put up in the twelfth and thirteenth centuries. In search of fortune, courageous citizens of Novgorod struck out far beyond the stone ridge of the Urals. By the eleventh century Novgorod was already ruling over territories that now make up Karelia and Archangel Region. In 1174 Novgoroders travelled along the Oka, the Volga and the Kama until they reached the Vyatka River. After some skirmishing, they came to the mouth of the Khlynovets River, where they put up a small fort, which they called Khlynov. Possibly some Novgoroder then drew forth a clay image of the great goddess, the Protectress of the Hearth, to offer prayers of thanks for safe arrival.

In these new territories Novgoroders established their own way of life, customs and rules, jealously preserving them through the centuries. They had no feudal lords and issues of war and alliance were discussed and decided by the "veche", the common council. No wonder furious Moscow boyars angrily termed these obstreperous folk "the thieves of Khlynov".

They also preserved the customs and religious rites of their ancestors. Generation after generation moulded clay images of the Protectress of the Hearth and celebrated the festive holiday of the Sun-God in spring. On every May 23, as the chronicles tell us, the common folk assembled "to dance and chant sundry heathen songs".

In 1418, the boyars of Moscow sought to take advantage of this care-free merriment and persuaded Anfal Nikitin, governor of Ustyug, and his son Nestor, to fall unawares on the people of Khlynov on this festive night.

All through the dark night on the eve of the festival, Ustyug troops stole up on Khlynov. But, just as they were about to storm the gates and walls of the town, the sentinels gave the alarm, and soon the tocsin tolled in warning. It was a bloody battle. Though the people of Khlynov put the enemy to rout, there was mourning in many a home in the town.

May 23 became a day of commemoration of the brave men slain in this cruel battle. From early morning on, the townsfolk would chant masses for the dead; towards evening, following the heavy drinking of a wake, celebrations of the Sun-God's holiday started, to last, with "whistling, booing and howling", as the chronicler put it, for as long as three whole days in some years.

It was to mark this festival that the craftsmen moulded their clay symbols of the Sun-God, the three-headed horses and their earthenware images of the Protectress of the Hearth, and also produced an abundance of clay and birch-bark whistles and clappers.

Though the populace of Khlynov escaped serfdom, and thus partially succeeded in preserving the ancient rites and customs—they were still celebrat-

Vyatka clay toys. Long ago the two-headed horse was the symbol of the Sund-God.

Clay toys from Tula Region. Similar to Vyatka toys, only more archaic in execution

 ing May 23 at the turn of this century—they failed to resist the Church. By 1780, when the town, by a whim of Catherine II was renamed Vyatka, the pagan holiday of spring had already been fully swaddled in the stuffy vestments of the Orthodox Church.

Read now a description of this festival given by Alexander Herzen, who was exiled to Vyatka in the mid-1830s.

"Some fifty versts away from Vyatka is the place where the wonder-working icon of Nikolai of Khlynov appeared to the Novgoroders. The Novgoroders had taken the icon with them when they founded Khlynov (Vyatka), but it vanished to reappear on the Great River some fifty versts from Vyatka; the Novgoroders carried it back again, vowing though to take it in ceremony down to the Great River every year were it to remain; this apparently occurs on May 23. That is the main summer holiday in Vyatka Province... Tens of thousands of people, from near and far, wait for the icon's appearance on the Great River. There they mill in vast numbers around one small village; strangest of all is that crowds of unbaptised Votyaks, Cheremyses and even Tatars, come to pray before the icon.

"Indeed, the festival is purely pagan in manifestation. At the foot of the monastery wall, Votyaks and Russians offer sheep and calves for sacrifice. They are slaughtered at once and the meat is dressed and sanctified."

During the 30s and 40s of the past century, Polish revolutionaries and progressive Russian intellectuals were exiled to Vyatka. Western and metropolitan fashions, never seen before in this remote backwoods, turned the local "aristocracy" green with envy. Soon their wives and daughters donned fashionable dress, which they had cut in their own manner. This hodge-podge of provincial philistinism and Parisian fashion presented a most amusing sight. No wonder, craftsmen produced for one of their spring festivals hundreds of sundry miniatures of the local snobs in their "stylish" clothes—tightly corseted ladies with a host of flounces, frills, ribbons and bows on their gowns and top-hatted "gents" in frock coats of incredible patterns.

This was by no means the first attempt to caricature the wealthy classes. Vyatka had a long-standing custom, in conformity with which the daughters of the rich went down to the pond for water after Sunday morning service. Togged out in all their finery, they seemed to float along like so many peahens, as the prospective bridegrooms lining the road and pondside, took critical stock of the brides-to-be. This custom is mirrored in the handiwork of the folk craftsmen, who produced the figure of "Water Carrier"—a young woman dressed in the broad, traditionally bell-shaped skirt in a large gaily-checkered pattern, that was set off by a small frilly apron. She also had a yellow blouse, a crimson bonnet, and several strands of beads wound round her full white throat. The yoke was bright green studded with tiny squares of gold leaf, while the pails themselves were orange.

Manufacture of these clay toys reached its zenith by the mid-nineteenth century. The inhabitanst of an entire neighbourhood were busily occupied moulding, drying and painting them. According to a local census of 1856, Vyatka had 59 families of toy makers, all of whom lived across the river in the neighbourhood of Dymkovo—which bestowed on the toys the still current name of the Dymkovo toy. The jealously preserved secrets of the craft were handed down in the family, from generation to generation.

In summer the members of the household would go out to the meadows and pastures in the vicinity and to the river to bring back red loam and fine sand. The loam was soaked in water, mixed with sand, and thoroughly kneaded by hand. By late autumn, when field work was over, the entire family, both young and old, occupied themselves with the making of these figures, producing them in batches. Such a toy as the "Water Carrier", for instance, would be made as follows: one member of the family would make a hundred or two of the bell-shaped skirts, another the arms and shoulders, a third the bonneted head, and a fourth the yoke and pails. The parts would then be joined together, a damp rag being used to rub the seams.

The batch would then be set out for several days to dry. Meanwhile, the family would start making a new batch—this time a horseman, or a nurse with child, or a stylishly dressed lady.

When dry, the figures were placed in the ordinary type of Russian stove, where they were fired for some three or four hours, the duration being determined by rule of thumb. It was a case of hit or miss: if the figure was taken out too early it crumbled; if taken out too late, the ground coat would fail to take. After the firing process, the toy was bathed two or three times in a pail of crushed and sifted chalk dissolved in milk. This gave the figure an even thin ground of white, which was excellent for the paint.

The painted doll would then be thoroughly coated with egg white and have tiny squares or lozenges of gold leaf glued on for brilliance. The finished

Clay toys from Kargopol in Northern Russia. Far more primitive in execution than the Vyatka toys

 product was then put on the shelf to stay there until the jobber, who paid only some thirty or forty kopeks a hundred, came.

Sometimes the craftsman tried to simplify his task. However, he would fail to outsmart the jobber, who would at once unctuously note:

"The lady's dress is plainer, which means you spent less time and energy on it. So I'll pay you twenty kopeks a hundred, instead of thirty."

One fine day a certain shrewd fellow suggested casting the dolls from plaster-of-Paris in moulds. This was successful, at first, the work being done much more rapidly and with less labour. The craftsmen were jubilant, thinking that now they would at last be able to extricate themselves from penury, even at the cost of sacrificing esthetic values.

This time it was the customer who failed to appreciate the innovation. On plaster-of-Paris the paint lost its previous sparkle. An unsold inventory of a host of dressy ladies, nurses, and horsemen, all alike as two peas, piled up.

Towards the close of the nineteenth century, the industry fell into complete apathy. The craftsmen scattered in search of a livelihood. Only two or three old women continued to while away the winter evenings, making bizarre-looking figures for the May festival.

The 1917 October Revolution swept away everything that had tended to degrade the talented artist and turn him into a penniless artisan. However, the many problems that arose could not be solved overnight. The surviving craftsmen found themselves at the crossroads. While, on the one hand, they were now able to create freely, being no longer tied to the jobber, on the other hand, they were worried whether there would be, in the new conditions, any demand for these gaily coloured clay dolls and toy whistles.

This state of flux may have persisted for a long time had it not been for the artist A. A. Denshin, a passionate, unselfish enthusiast of the Dymkovo toy.

In that time of hunger and ruin, when long lines queued up for the meagre bread ration in Moscow, and all that people had to light their rooms with was a sputtering wick lamp, he wrote book after book to popularise the inimitable beauty of the ancient Vyatka craft. Warming his numbed fingers over the make-shift stove in his cold, bleak room, he painted in by hand all the drawings in each printed copy.

Later, he went to Dymkovo to persuade the few surviving craftsmen that it was necessary to keep the flame alive. His efforts were not in vain. The ancient craft experienced a renascence.

Early 20th-century Kargopol clay toys

Years later, in 1936, the Government commissioned Dymkovo artists to decorate a pavilion at the USSR Agricultural Exhibition. In 1937, the French Minister of Trade personally signed the certificate of honour which the World Fair awarded to the old craftswomen of Dymkovo.

At the 1939 World Fair in New York the eminent art scholars on the jury unanimously awarded gold medals to the Vyatka toy makers.

Today the Dymkovo toy making shop is housed in the new building of the Artists' House, right in the centre of Kirov—in 1934 Vyatka was renamed after this celebrated Soviet statesman. However, nothing has changed as far as the technique is concerned. The red loam is still mixed with sand and still thoroughly kneaded by hand, as it was some three or even five centuries ago.

Nor has the toy's vivid coat of colour changed.
The girl artist still paints the old bright circles and squares.
On the chest of the snow-white, three-headed horse,
she will deftly outline a radiating crimson circle,
totally unaware, just as was her distant predecessor,
that this circle symbolises the pagan Sun-God.
The veterans who revived the craft in Soviet times—they
are Anna Mezrina, Zoya Penkina, Yevdokia Koshkina,
and Yelena Kos-Denshina—have placed its secrets
in safe, reliable, young hands.
We are, unfortunately, ignorant of the names of craftsmen
of the past. However, a comparison distinctly shows that
the figures made nowadays still possess the old form and
colouring, and have lost nothing of the old charm.
Every month, several hundred of these colourful clay dolls,
which are so appealing by virtue of their unusual combination
of an inner realism wedded to a fairy-tale form, are
shipped from Kirov to shops both in the USSR and abroad,
where they are snapped up by connoisseur and layman alike.

LACQUERS

hose fragile ebony teacups that are gilded inside, silvery-green ash containers, gaily coloured gleaming black snuffboxes, and cherry-red vases are all lacquered objects, made of a material that seems to resemble wood, bone and cardboard all wrapped up in one. For a long time Russian scholars believed the first home-made lacquered articles were produced only at the tail end of the eighteenth century and were fashioned after the German product. However, some thing that happened during the last war made the experts change their minds.

Nazi troops had reached the walls of Leningrad and had captured Peterhof. Its fabulous palaces, lovely park and beautiful fountains were savagely destroyed with typical nazi barbarity. Even Peterhof's oldest building, the Palace of Mon Plaisir, which Peter the Great had erected to honour the Russian naval victory of Gangut, was not spared.

For two hundred and twenty years, Peter the Great's country palace had aroused delight and amazement among aesthetes. It was famed for its lacquered room, where old Chinese and Japanese tableware was kept. The walls of this small room were inset with black lacquered panels which Chinese craftsmen had decorated with drawings in fine, wavy lines of silver and gold. On the day Soviet fighting men liberated Peterhof, they found Mon Plaisir a smoking skeleton. Its scarred, flaking walls and empty eyepits in place of windows stared down at them. The lacquered room no longer existed. Only after painstaking search, did the Leningrad scholar M. Tikhomirova discover, by a fluke, in a nazi pillbox, four of the 92 lacquer panels which had once adorned the room.

CONSUMMATE CRAFTSMANSHIP

As soon as the war was over, the Soviet Government took a decision to restore all destroyed historical monuments. Peterhof, along with Mon Plaisir, was rebuilt. But a locked door hid the denuded walls of the nazi ransacked lacquered room. The problem that now occupied the minds of restoration experts was whether anyone could reproduce the lost panels. Tikhomirova called in one more consultant. This was Merited Art Worker of the Russian Federation, A. V. Kotukhin, a Palekh-born artist, who came to Leningrad specially from Ivanovo Region.

Fingering his bushy grey moustache and knitting his thick eyebrows, the old man meticulously examined the surviving panels, all but testing them with his teeth. Then he declared, in a voice ringing with conviction:

"Russian craftsmen made these panels. They are painted on limewood boards, like icons."

The astonishment that greeted this pronouncement was of the sort a person experiences, when, after hunting the better half of a day for presumably lost eyeglasses, suddenly realises they are on the tip of his nose. So back to the archives the experts went.

A thorough search revealed several curious documents among the papers of Peter the Great's Construction Committee. These included the Tsar's letter to the architect Brownstein, commissioning him to build at the earliest date a room to contain porcelain, and the contract the architect himself had signed with craftsmen Ivan Tikhanov and Ivan Polyakov to do Chinese lacquer work for Peterhof.

The painters took out their contract on June 26, 1720. Almost two years later to a day, on June 8, 1722, they and their apprentices signed the pay roll. This small room in the imperial palace at Peterhof had, as was mentioned earlier, 92 lacquered panels. In the flickering light of the wax candles of the massive candelabra, the tiny Chinese figures, which were etched in gold and silver against a black background, seemed to spring to life. Nimble peddlers deftly wended their way across the humpbacked bridges, skittish beauties languidly fanned themselves, and staid mandarins strolled through the miniature gardens. So when the decision was taken to restore these panels, craftsmen from the old Russian village of Palekh, which is located in what is now Ivanovo Region, were naturally assigned this task.

Palekh

THE ARRIVING traveller cannot see the village as yet, but the pointed tip of a campanile peeping out from behind the yellow squares of ripening rye and the bottle-green barrier of thickets tells him that Palekh lies yonder.

This church, or rather the Church generally, is representative of all of

Palekh's past. Many old Russian temples redound to the glory of the painters
of Palekh, who were famed for their icons.

Though we do not know the exact time the village was founded, a letter addressed in the mid-17th century to the Moscow painter Semyon Ushakov speaks of villagers of Palekh who bartered for eggs and onions icons they themselves had painted.

The secrets of the craft were handed down from father to son. However, though they possessed great talent, the peasant artists lived in constant penury and ignorance. They invested the customary features of the saints with some-

'ire-Bird" snuff-box. By . Kotukhin, foundation ember of Palekh lac- erware artel

 thing all their own, producing inimitable masterpieces, the fame of which had spread far outside the country towards the close of the eighteenth century.

First to display a serious scholarly interest in Palekh handiwork was a foreigner, the great German poet and thinker Wolfgang Goethe. Chancing to see several Russian icons he realised that this was an entire realm of art which had a long history and of which Westerners were utterly ignorant.

In 1813, in a letter to the Russian Government, he noted that in Suzdal and its neighbourhood, in Vladimir Province, images were made which served not so much as objects of religious worship, as the expression of a creative urge.

Goethe wished to know how long this industry had been established, whether there were any Greek icons serving as prototypes, whether there were any eminent artists among the Suzdal icon painters, and whether all the work conformed only to the old, sacred style, or whether other modern artistic objects were made there.

In his reply the governor of Vladimir Province said Suzdal painters were not producing any other modern, artistic objects. He detailed all the icon painters' villages, singling out Palekh. Describing the work of the icon painters, he named the two best artists — notably the Kourtsevs, Andrei and Ivan. He also mailed two smaller items by the Kourtsevs to St. Petersburg. Still extant in the old church that towers up in the centre of the village, are some lovely icons, whose stern "saintly" visages are lost in a flaming brilliance of crimsons, greens, browns and golds.

Museum exhibits clearly show that by the beginning of this century Palekh painting had died out. Taking over the icon painting industry, the capitalist split up a once integral, artistically comprehensive task into several separate mechanical operations. The come-down was so obvious, that the great Russian writer, Anton Chekhov, who had close ties with Palekh—his mother was born in the village of Sergeyevo three kilometres away from Palekh, and some of her relatives were icon painters themselves—noted in 1901, that as an art icon painting was already making its exit and that Palekh would never get back on its feet again.

Today, the old church serves as an anteroom to the nearby, separate new two-storey building of the museum. The reverberating gloomy church presents a sharp contrast to the sunny capacious rooms of the museum with their

Early Palekh lacquer miniature by Ivan Golikov, the father of Palekh ware

gleaming glass showcases. Instead of grim-visaged "saints", one is lost in a gay confusion of miniatures, that sparkle with optimism and mirth. This is the Palekh of Soviet times.

When the 1917 October Revolution came, the demand for icons fell off. In search of a livelihood, the painters took any job that came their way. The more timid produced painted wooden toys; the go-getters flocked to Moscow in search of fortune.

 The kind lady of fortune indeed turned her face their way. This was no whim of chance, though, but the logical outcome of a persistent quest. While in Moscow, the craftsman Ivan Golikov happened to see the painted lacquered boxes, caskets and the like exhibited at the Arts and Handicrafts Museum. "I couldn't get those boxes out of my mind," Golikov recollected later. "And I thought to myself that if our fellow villagers did the same sort of thing, no

"Battle Scene," a favourite theme with Golikov

"Troika." Early piece by I. Golikov. Palekh. 1927

one would have to worry about the money and there would be no more grumbling and groaning."

When the curator learned that the artist who asked him for the necessary materials, was nothing but an erstwhile icon painter, he showed him the door. This did not deter Golikov, however. He dug up an old papier-mâché photo-tray, cut off the bottom and got down to work. On the black background he painted in gold and silver the bizarre beasts and birds he has once painted in the icon "John the Baptist in the Wilderness". When ready, he took it to the museum. This time he got what he wanted. He was given smooth black caskets and boxes and his painting was put on display. So did a new art come into its own.

Several months later, the one-time icon painters of Palekh established a co-operative of their own. Its first chairman was the experienced painter Alexander Kotukhin. One of his first pieces, the "Fire-Bird" box, is currently on view at Moscow's Tretyakov Art Gallery. It depicts the young fairy-tale hero who crossed mountains to steal a feather from the Fire-Bird which lived in a magic orchard. One can admire without end the weaving, exotic ferns, the scintillating brightly coloured shrubs and bushes, and the exquisitely delineated folds of the hero's clothes. Kotukhin did not pick this theme at random. In his eyes the fabulous bird symbolised free and joyous creative endeavour.

The initial gold-crimson creations of the painters were only the first glimpses of a distant, but quite attainable, goal. Now it was necessary to introduce modern themes. Heaven knows how long it would have taken the new Palekh to achieve full blossom, had it not been for the writer Maxim Gorky's effective assistance.

Curiously enough, Palekh has throughout its history invariably attracted such great men of literature, as Goethe, Chekhov, and Gorky.

Gorky was first introduced to Palekh when, at the age of fourteen, he was apprenticed to the icon painting shop of the merchant Salabanov, who himself hailed from this village. There he made friends with Palekh painters, whom he subsequently described as "kind people".

Though it was half a century before Gorky revisited Palekh, he always followed every advance it made, rejoicing at its achievements. In 1927, while in faraway Sorrento,

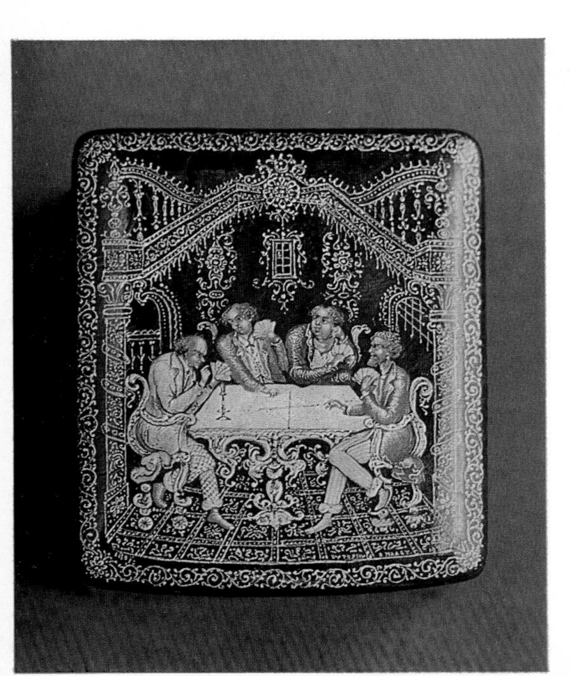

"Card-players." Matchbox size. Miniature by D. Butorin

Painted Palekh papier-mâché platter. By I. Markichev, veteran craftsman

the proletarian author described the new creative path of the Palekh painters as "one of those minor miracles that the revolution works" and as "testimony to the awakening of creative energies among the masses of working folk".

A rustic scene. Palekh

"One needs merely compare," he wrote elsewhere, "the work of the icon painters of Palekh, Kholui, and Mstera before the Revolution, with their present work to be amazed indeed by their great strides forward. This is quite likely one of the most noteworthy leaps from the 'necessity' of slave labour to the freedom of creativity."

Maxim Gorky came back to Russia in the spring of 1928. The first thing he did, while still on the train, was to talk to *Izvestia*'s editor-in-chief about taking up a collection to help the painters of Palekh. They soon got ten thousand rubles to outfit a new workshop, and crates of books on the history of the visual arts.

Defending this new art from its sundry sorry critics, the writer exclaimed in a voice that rang out to every end of the country: "Palekh art quite deserves a broader and more knowing evaluation than given now."

On September 25, 1932, a deputation from the village presented the great writer with a modest token of their appreciation of his kind and comradely help. Inside a large casket, with scenes from Gorky's short story "Old Woman Izergil", painted by the leading artist, D. Butorin, lay a Palekh co-operative certificate of honourable membership.

"Thrashing Flax." Small lacquered box by I. Bakanov. 1924

This illustrious man of letters had helped the folk artists to snare and tame the fabulous Fire-Bird. Meanwhile, at the co-operative's museum, which was also started on Gorky's initiative, there scintillated with all the colours of the rainbow, masterpieces by Palekh painters of every generation. One will never fail to be amazed at the generosity with which nature has endowed the Palekh painters. There does not seem to be a single visual art to which they are unable to contribute some novelty of their own.

In the museum, one's eye is sure to be drawn at once to the busts of the founders and veterans of the handicraft, I. Vakurov, A. Vatagin, A. Dydykin, D. Butorin, and N. Zinoviev. The heads, incidentally, were done by Nikolai Dydykin, who is himself of Palekh stock.

Above the busts and glass showcases, in which against their background of black lacquer, Palekh miniatures shine like precious gems set in gold and silver filigree, are several huge canvases. Both mural paints and their descendants—Palekh artists once painted the walls of the Kremlin's world-famous Granovitaya Palata (Palace of Facets)—have repeatedly essayed easel painting, but observing the centuries-old manner of the icon painters. Next to these canvases, one finds ordinary Palekh painted glassware, china saucers, ancient parchment and sheets of drawing paper, all radiating a sparkling iridescence.

Most of these paintings are the product of the imagination and talent of that great genius of Palekh, Ivan Golikov, whom the writer Yefim Vikhrev, Palekh's chronicler, has compared with Michelangelo himself.

Golikov unleashed a veritable whirlwind of brilliant colour in his many battle and troika scenes and also gave those inimitable illustrations to the *The Lay of Igor's Host*, which comprise the acme and heart of the new Palekh art. He would have never achieved what he did but for the Revolution, which threw the doors to art wide open before him. Though it is impossible to imitate Golikov, just as it is impossible to copy the creations of any genius, all succeeding generations of Palekh painters have been infected with his fervour and catholic range of quest.

Golikov, together with many of his fellow painters who co-operated with him in starting the new handicraft, died long ago, while the artists of the second generation have retired on pension. Their place has been taken by representatives of the third, and even fourth, generations, including women, something unprecedented in icon painting history. In addition to their lacquered miniatures, Palekh artists also do wonderful book illustrations, decorate the interior of new palaces of culture and boarding schools, and paint stage sets.

Palekh painting is at present part and parcel of everyday life. The great changes the country has undergone since the 1917 Revolution clamour for artistic presentation and Palekh painters well realise that. Whereas in their first twenty years, the co-operative, for the most part, did unparalleled miniatures based on folk songs, fairy-tales, Pushkin's poetry, and Gorky's stories, of late, more and more compositions dealing with present-day Soviet reality have appeared.

No novelty comes of its own accord. It has to be discovered and ensconced. Consequently mistakes, even setbacks, are quite possible. In their searchings some painters lost their sense of decorativeness and, blindly copied easel paintings, forgetting the traditional, inimitable features of their own handicraft. However, when one perseveres, success is sure to follow setbacks. Strangely enough for the old, but logically enough for the new Palekh, it was a representative of the fair sex who gained one of these successes. Ingenious Tamara Zubkova was first to base several interesting compositions on popular Soviet songs. She is no lone ranger. Exhibited at various museums are miniatures on modern topics by such experienced painters as A. Kotukhin, A. Zaitsev, A. Kurkin and G. Melnikov, who have won fine repute both inside and outside the USSR. Incidentally, it was these pupils of the founders of the co-operative who worked a minor miracle, reproducing the lacquered room at Mon Plaisir. Drawing inspiration from an ancient Oriental carpet preserved at the Hermitage, Nikolai Zinoviev's team of Palekh artists again peopled the black-lacquered walls of the small room with figures in gold and silver. And again, as two hundred years ago, nimble peddlers glide over humpbacked bridges, languid beauties fan themselves and pompous mandarins stroll sedately. The only change is of the stork, whose repeated image fringes the carpet. Palekh craftsmen have transformed it into the Russian fairy-tale Fire-Bird.

Palekh artists are justly proud of their handiwork, which has taken more than one medal at more than one exhibition abroad. Soviet newspapers report the titles and government decorations awarded to the creators of the superb lacquered miniatures and magic theatrical decor. In bookshops one will find publications illustrated by the masters of Palekh.

In its new garb this century-old art has become handsomer still, and is known to hundreds of thousands, perhaps even millions, of people. In short, it has achieved immortality. But one may legitimately ask: Since Palekh lacquers first appeared in 1924, only after Golikov had seen lacquered snuff boxes at the Museum of Arts and Handicrafts, who then made the original snuff boxes? And when and where?

The answer is to be found in the history of the peasant craftsmen of a village near Moscow called Fedoskino.

Fedoskino

IN 1844 a new book by M. N. Zagoskin, author of the then popular novel *Yuri Miloslavsky*, caused quite a stir among the Russian reading public. Book lovers eagerly snapped up the just published *Moscow and Its People. The Diaries of Bogdan Ilyich Belsky*.

Along with other entertaining anecdotes, the hero of Zagoskin's new book describes an incident that was supposed to have happened to a friend of his in Paris. "About to leave for Russia," he relates, "my friend decided to acquire a good paper snuff box in Paris. He made his choice and as he stood admiring it, most likely deplored the fact that we, in Russia, couldn't do such things. How amazed he was, when desirous of putting his purchase to the use it was intended, he found on the inner side of the lid the image of the twin-headed Russian eagle and the signature of the merchant Lukutin."

A glance through the time-yellowed pages of newspapers of the 1830s and 1840s will reveal the oft-recurring name of this merchant, now in an advertisement, now in a letter of commendation from a customer.

These old newspapers enable us to trace the history of his factory right back to the year 1824. To learn earlier details, however, we must resort to the archives.

Prior to 1818 the factory belonged to the merchant Korobov, who was Lukutin's father-in-law. Contemporaries of Korobov say that his products were extremely popular. In 1804, for instance, a total of 9,094 handpainted snuff boxes were sold in Russia.

Men of fashion in both Moscow and St. Petersburg marvelled at these ebony-tinted lacquered boxes. In the first place, they were lighter and cheaper than the habitual china article. The urban dandy would no doubt wonder, as he opened the lid to reveal the inner flame of red, where Korobov had learned the art of making so charming a thing.

The shrewd merchant had acquired the secret during his travels in Brunswick, Germany.

Returning to Russia in 1795, Korobov purchased Danilkovo, which was part of the village of Fedoskino, and caused his serfs to manufacture caskets and boxes that were based on foreign patterns. Very shortly, the ingenious Russian peasant, having mastered all the fine points, introduced some innovations of his own, thus tending to improve upon the German or, rather, Oriental product, as Europeans were first introduced to lacquers in the sixteenth century when enterprising traders brought back from the East exotic vases, caskets and tableware of some unknown material.

Though the ingenious artisans tried hard, they failed to reproduce these lovely objects. Europe lacked the tree that grew in such abundance in Asia, and whose sap provided gifted Oriental craftsmen with their basic material. The artisan made a fragile skeleton for his future casket or vase from wood, or sometimes from metal. Then coat after coat of a peculiar kind of resin was added. The craftsman sometimes tinted the resin. The coating could be made of any thickness and then one or another pattern was carved in it.

During that same sixteenth century, Europe was first introduced to the ware of Persian craftsmen whose caskets and boxes were made of several layers of glued paper that was subsequently coated with a mixture of glue and chalk, then painted, and finally covered with a transparent varnish. Europeans soon mastered the art. However, the demand fell off just as quickly. Only quite recently scholars happened to find that the colours used in the Persian lacquer miniatures had been mixed with egg distemper and that the painting itself had been executed by the same methods which the painters of ancient Byzantium and the icon painters of Russia had applied so long ago.

Korobov's smart serfs glued together compressed sheets of cardboard, which they then boiled in flaxseed oil and oven dried. The resulting product was so sturdy and water-resistant that it could even be machined.

Every box made in this way was thoroughly polished, given a grounding and then varnished, in the same manner as icons—the sole difference being, that while Korobov's people used ordinary, cheap oils, the icon painters employed special paints mixed with the yoke of an egg. A picture or design would be painted on, after which the box would be given several coatings of lacquer, oven dried and fine-polished. The whole process took seventy days.

Shrewd Alexander Lukutin catered for every taste. The rich were offered cigarette boxes, caskets, and other objects with meticulously painted genre scenes and landscapes on the lids. Now and again the gleaming black top would be inlaid with mother-of-pearl or thin strips of silver or gold.

For the less well-to-do—petty officials, merchants and townsfolk—there were, at best, reproductions of famous masters, or, mostly, a rehash of a picture from some illustrated magazine.

However, in the same way that a talented musician imparts an original freshness to even a hackneyed composition, so did the serf painters give a new twist to their copies. As experience and mastery grew, the craftsman more and more frequently introduced scenes of a rustic nature as being closer to his mind and heart.

In coming decades historians and ethnographers will no doubt resort to Lukutin's boxes to learn about the life of Russia's peasants, artisans and townsfolk in the second half of the past century. A small casket having on its lid the picture of two artisans staidly sipping tea from saucers as the samovar on the table bubbles and hisses will reveal a great deal. It is a scene full of most interesting detail. It shows what the Tula samovar looked like in the 1870s and the viewer will note the cheap, china teapot with its painted bouquet of roses, the cut of the men's waistcoats and high boots, and even the characteristic hair style. The scenes of a peasant family out haymaking, or having dinner, as well as of tavern carousals and market episodes are all of great ethnographic and historical value, a value which will increase as the years pass.

Every historian interested in the development of capitalism in Russia will be able to learn much from Fedoskino, as the history of its development is most characteristic. Beginning at the close of the eighteenth century as a small workshop, it gradually grew into a large manufactory. However, when, in the second half of the nineteenth century, Lukutin had to compete with cheap factory-made quantity-produced china, metal and woodware, he went bankrupt and in 1904 his establishment was shut down.

Meanwhile, the story of the Fedoskino painters themselves is testimony to the great affection the ordinary Russian entertains for the beauty of his homeland; it is a paean to perseverance and patience.

At the turn of the twentieth century Fedoskino was Europe's only centre still making artistic lacquers, the craft having long since become genuinely national, genuinely Russian. Its demise impoverished national culture.

In 1910, several highly skilled painters and craftsmen, who had worked at Lukutin's manufactory, set up their own co-operative. This ambitious project caused them many worries. They had to mortgage their belongings, abase themselves before prospective clients and rebuild the workshop which unknown vandals had burned down. Nevertheless, they embraced these tribulations to preserve the craft and save their families from slow death by starvation.

Though unaware of it, the Fedoskino painters had adopted the same policy the bone carvers of Tobolsk and the wood carvers of Bogorodskoye were pursuing at the time. They also mortgaged their property, and suffered privations and humiliations, to preserve folk art treasures.

Later, the roads of all three were to cross more than once. Indeed, today every exhibition, inside or outside the country, will certainly display lacquers next to yellowish ivories and carved wooden miniatures. All three co-operatives

Tartan decor. Fedoskino lacquerware of papier-mâché. Late 19th century

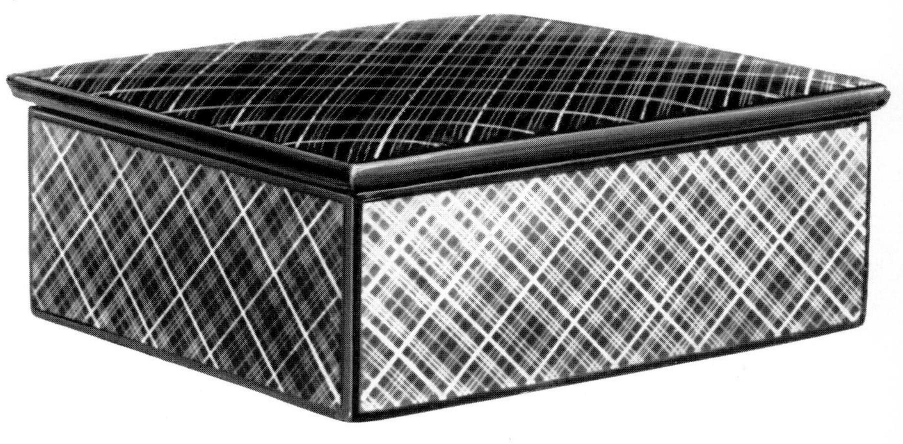

 are equally entitled to be proud of their achievements attested by the many certificates of honour and medals won at shows and fairs.

More than 150 years have elapsed since Korobov started his manufactory. Life has changed beyond recognition. Today man has clever machines to help him. Electronic computers discharge some functions of the brain, while highly complex equipment makes machine parts by itself, at man's bidding. There are artificial limbs that both look and operate like natural ones. However, nothing has changed in the lacquer polishing process. Just like his forefathers 150 years ago, the craftsman of today spends hours polishing the lid with his warm palms, as only that imparts the peculiar, translucent brilliance.

Hand-polishing, however, is all that remains of old-time Fedoskino. The log cabin that once housed the first workshop, has long been replaced by a fine brick building that stands amidst an excellently appointed residential neighbourhood. Some three hundred pastmasters of the craft have taken over from the old artists who created the famous troika, round-dance and tea-drinking scenes. The prizes and medals awarded at recent international exhibitions redound to the credit of a new generation of artists.

Fedoskino is on the upgrade today. The fine compositions on modern themes or on themes borrowed from Russian folk tales, are executed by such top-notch artists as V. Lipitsky, S. Rogatov, M. Pashinin and M. Chizhov—to mention a few. Each new achievement is doubly appreciated not only by the Fedoskino painters themselves, but also by all aesthetes, as the ingenious craftsmen of this Russian village have not only preserved a wonderful art, but have also been godfathers to new lacquer industries appearing in Soviet times.

Mstera

BY THE mid-eighteenth century there were only three icon painting centres left in Russia. Only in Palekh, Mstera and the small village of Kholui were icons still painted strictly according to the age-old rules of composition and colouring. Nevertheless, there was an appreciable distinction in style between the three.

Palekh produced for the most part costly icons that were extremely popular with aristocrats and opulent industrialists, and whose gay confusion of colour sparkled, gem-like, against a background of gold or silver.

Meanwhile, Mstera sought to emulate the fifteenth and sixteenth century austerity. Its icons were greatly favoured by Russia's Old Believers' sect. To curry favour with their wealthy clients, at the outset Mstera craftsmen meticu-

"Tea-Drinking" scene. Papier-mâché box. Oils on silver background. By I. Semyonov. 1934

lously copied Old Masters; later they painted their own icons in the same manner. There was not a single old school of icon painting in Russia, which they failed to imitate. By the turn of the twentieth century Mstera had become the country's biggest supplier of "antique" icons. Every year hundreds of itinerant peddlers hawked thousands of Mstera icons all over the country. In remote, backwoods villages they snapped up for a song old, begrimed, peeling icons, which Mstera craftsmen would restore and resell at a great profit to antique lovers in Moscow and St. Petersburg.

 Decades later V. N. Ovchinnikov, an erstwhile icon painter, observed: "Mstera craftsmen were so good at copying old icons, that quite often, the dating of a newly painted one would baffle the export. Great pains were taken to restore ancient icons. Sometimes more than half was added anew to the few surviving patches. Nevertheless, the icon would be shown at a museum as one that had remained intact.

"In Mstera this copying of the old Novgorod and Stroganov schools, among others, was brought to consummate perfection. No craftsmen from any other icon painting village could hold a candle to the Mstera painters."

Another line in Mstera was the faking of antique icons. They faked everything, the aged wood, the yellowed, cracked, coat of drying oil, and the style of the Greek, Novgorod or Moscow schools. With an "authenticity" guarantee, the sham icon would then be palmed off on a collector or even museum. Only after the Revolution, did one of their swindles come to light, when art scholars were first able to catalogue in detail all the treasures of the Leningrad Winter Palace. When the results were published, scholars, who had only recently waxed enthusiastic over the Tsar's personal collection of some three hundred icons, found themselves in an embarrassing predicament. All the three hundred supposedly authentic creations of anonymous Russian icon painters of the twelfth-fifteenth centuries had been cleverly faked in the early 20th century by Mstera craftsmen.

Mstera was famed not only for its icons. It also provided the tens of thousands of broadside prints, with pictures based on themes borrowed from folk tales and songs, that were hawked throughout the length and breadth of the country. These broadsides, or "lubki", as they were called in Russia, were printed from a wooden, metal or stone master-block. This industry was run by the self-taught Mstera archaeologist and historian, Golyshev, whose house still stands in Mstera. The drawings were done by the local icon painters and coloured in a slap-dash fashion, in purples, yellows, blues, or reds, by their women and children, who didn't give a tinker's damn if half a face were blue and half white.

Mstera at the time was a cross between town and village. Ramshackle wooden cottages with bleary-eyed, ground-low windows hobnobbed with fine two-storey brick mansions, in whose grounds stood squat storehouses, surrounded by wooden fences or even stone walls, behind which, at holiday time, the local rich staged geese fights, their favourite form of entertainment. In the storehouses the employer kept the goods he drew upon to pay his workers. Their worth was often assessed at higher than market value, but the craftsman had to take them at the price, because he was usually paid on Saturday, when his wife and children would be expecting him impatiently.

Another common "pay envelope" in Mstera was vodka. After the job was done, the employer would broach a cask of vodka for the painters. As a rule, this triggered off a debauch of several days, during which abusive recriminations and blows would often be exchanged. Later, the employer would deduct the cost of the vodka from the icon painters' earnings.

However, despite slave labour from four in the morning till seven at night, and despite the sordid, savage drunkenness, a few of the talented artists made good.

Thus, Nikolai Klykov became instructor at the Stroganov School of Arts, while Alexander Bryagin and Alexander Kotyagin excelled in restoration work at museums in St. Petersburg and the churches of Pskov and Novgorod. These three men shared much in common. During the October 1917 Revolution, the two former icon painters, Bryagin and Kotyagin, served in the Red Guards and stormed the Winter Palace. Later on, they went to Siberia as commissars of food-requisitioning units, and fought in the Civil War against kulak bands, before they finally came back to the new Mstera. It was these three top-notch artists who, in the twenties, laid the groundwork for Soviet Mstera's future fame.

Soon after the Revolution, Mstera craftsmen switched to making painted, turned wooden toys and the painting of oilcloth, kerchiefs, tea caddies, and sugar bowls earning themselves the nickname of "the doll makers of Mstera" in the neighbouring villages.

Klykov, Bryagin and Kotyagin decided to put an end to these taunts. Before the Revolution they had heard much about the Fedoskino painters. At one time even Alexander Bryagin had kept the tobacco for his fat, home-rolled cigarettes in a lacquered snuffbox which had come from the Lukutin manufactory. The three craftsmen first essayed lacquered miniatures in 1923 but were not successful, the result being too reminiscent of an icon. The black lacquer was totally obscured by an icon-like coat of gold. The houses and general background landscape had been copied from an old miniature, and instead of modern, flesh-and-blood people, "saints" in lay dress dominated the scene.

 The three realised that lacquer painting had laws of its own, which could be mastered only by dedicated effort.

Two art scholars, Prof. A. V. Bakushinsky and V. M. Vasilenko came to Mstera to help its craftsmen tackle the new tasks. More than once did grey-headed artists dash their handiwork to the floor in fits of petulance, on hearing Bakushinsky say again that it wouldn't do. The next day they would turn up, like so many repentant schoolchildren, to resume their studies until they again hurled an unfinished task to the floor.

In 1932, the Proletarian Art Co-operative of Mstera started quantity production of papier-mâché lacquered objects, decorated with painted miniatures. The service Bryagin, Klykov and Kotyagin rendered is that they not only fathered a craft novel to Mstera, but also enabled the newly-established co-operative to develop its own style.

Mstera lacquers differ greatly in their landscapes, from Palekh miniatures. The Palekh landscape is conventional, the trees and bushes being relegated to the background and the black serving for blue sky. In Mstera miniatures, however, the thickets, ponds and blue heavens with their fleecy clouds, all play their own necessary and significant part. The meadows, groves and streams in Mstera's neighbourhood are so attractive and lovely that its artists could not but paint them in accurate detail.

It was the broadsides that gave Mstera craftsmen their penchant for depicting life around them realistically, for painting genre scenes. Moreover, a knowledge of ancient manuscripts and their illuminations and vignettes stimulated the appearance of a novel ornamental pattern unknown in either Palekh or Fedoskino. Finely pencilled on the gleaming black background is the flexuous golden thread of a fabulous herb coupled with the long stalks of exotic flowers. Now merging in one tangle, now radiating, they then give place to a bright splotch of brilliant colour.

Paradoxically enough, the inimitable manner of each of these talented painters served to engender a common style in the Mstera miniature. Klykov contributed lyrical pensiveness, Bryagin, decorativeness, and Kotyagin, compositional austerity. To these three we must add Y. V. Yurin, an unexcelled master of ornamental patterns, I. N. Morozov and V. N. Ovchinnikov, painters of the second and third generations, and even the young graduates from the art school in the white-colonnaded mansion next door.

In the period since Mstera started anew in Soviet times, a number of painters

Mstera lacquered box of papier-mâché. By Lev Fomichev. 1958

possessing individuality and styles of their own, have come to the fore. At the top of the list is Merited Art Worker of the Russian Federation Ivan Fomichov.

This erstwhile icon painter—he used to paint the entire icon except for the faces of the saints—is today a deputy to the Regional Soviet and one of the most popular people in Mstera. One need only go to the marketplace—which is hemmed in on three sides by the monastery wall and brick houses and the old low arcades, and ask anyone where he lives, to hear:

"Why, man, climb that street up the hill. Right to the very end, almost. You'll find his house at No. 80, on the right-hand side."

Fomichov is a confirmed bachelor, convinced that you can't have both art and family. On his table one will see, beside a glass of tea, both a gold-embossed tome of *The History of the Arts* and a slender volume of verse by Pushkin, while the sugar bowl and teapot mingle with several small jars of paint. With Fomichov the process of creation is a long, continuous one. Whether angling, picking mushrooms or pottering around in his small vegetable garden, the strenuous and at times subconscious mental process goes on storing away in the mind isolated gestures, silhouettes of trees and houses, and the elusive tints of a morning sky or honey-hued autumn leaves.

This seeming idleness may continue for a fortnight, until there comes the moment, when all the imagery and colour burst forth and the accumulated impressions spill out in veritable rainbow profusion to form the initial sketch of a new composition. Others are sure to follow, for all the different tints and clear-etched lines that spring from the mind never seem able to settle down to live in accord. Now one, now the other, will try to predominate. It takes artistry and skill to curb this multicoloured pandemonium. More sketches are made with one aspect emphasised and the other suppressed, until, finally, everything blends into harmony.

No wonder Fomichov is always so reluctant to show his sketches, though, on the other hand, he always willingly displays the finished article.

"No," he says, adamant, "you may beg me as much as you like, but I won't show you my sketches. Would you want me to stand here naked? Not on your life. How long does a piece take? Is that what you want to know? Well, it varies. Sometimes it takes a long time, sometimes it's quick. You never know. But, on the average I do 13-14 miniatures a year. However, you shouldn't be writing about me only. It's the factory, all our lacquer craft, you should write about. You see, we've got difficulties of our own, and they're quite formidable, too. For instance, we've got to stick to our own rules of the art. Besides presenting a composite theme, we must always remember that the decorative angle must be based on one common point of departure, so that the pictorial representation of people, animals, houses and trees blend into one ornamental rhythm.

"However, some of the younger folk," Fomichov continued, "forget we are not doing paintings for palaces or art galleries but a decorative ornamental object. Colour comes first. In the home every casket or box of ours must catch the eye with its brilliance. Then one will look closer at the picture. Only you can't copy everything as it is in life. You've got the camera for that. What you've got to do, is to look around, observing things as they are today, tomorrow and the day after that, and then put down the generalised impression.

"Those who fail today will some time realise where they went wrong. It's indifference that's really bad. Whenever I see such people I feel sad, because they aren't giving up all of themselves to art. They're like a used-up matchbox. You keep on striking a match but it won't catch light. A picture with no spark and flame in it, is simply drab and boring."

This was not the grumbling of an irascible old man, but an expression of his keen interest in the work he loved, the wish to see his factory make still better progress, and pass on experience and mastery to the younger generation.

"We must never forget that every piece we make is an ambassador for the country, both abroad and into the future," Fomichov concluded. "Take me here now, sitting and chatting with you. I've got my house slippers on and my jacket is all stained with paint. But if I went out, I'd get dressed up, with a white shirt and tie; so does an object of art go from the workshop as a guest to other homes. I expect you'll see pieces that I've done, all over the world. I've done things for Britain, Australia, France and the United States. Let them see what a gay, happy life we're leading, and let generations appreciate it too when they see our work."

Fomichov is not the only one who subscribes to such views. There are many famous painters in Mstera. Much of the credit for its well deserved success at international fairs is due to the Dmitrievs, husband and wife, to the miniature painters Y. Zonina and I. Balakin, and to the very gifted young Lev Fomichov, a pupil, but no relative, of Ivan Fomichov's.

As one takes an admiring look at these new creations, one clearly realises that both Mstera's present and future cannot be viewed in isolation from the magnificent collection of ancient icons at the local museum, the entrancing

expanses of meadows, the road leading
through the pine tree groves,
the autumn woods flaming red on the
horizon, and the roar of
an aircraft, which seems to zoom so low
that it might hit a tall
television aerial. Mstera's future has
an inseparable bond with
Russia's past and present. Its destiny,
like all of Russian folk art, cannot be
divorced from the life
of the country
generally. Therein lies the earnest of its
future achievements and further
flowering.

TO THE READER

Progress Publishers would be glad to have your opinion of this book, its translation and design and any suggestions you may have for future publications.

Please send your comments to 21, Zubovsky Boulevard, Moscow, USSR.

Printed in the Union of Soviet Socialist Republics